CAMPING,
Simple and Cheap

CAMPING,
Simple and Cheap

Patrick J. Smith

iUniverse, Inc.
New York   Bloomington

Camping, Simple and Cheap

iUniverse books may be ordered through booksellers or by contacting:

iUniverse
1663 Liberty Drive
Bloomington, IN 47403
www.iuniverse.com
1-800-Authors (1-800-288-4677)

ISBN: 978-1-4502-2071-2 (pbk)
ISBN: 978-1-4502-2072-9 (ebk)

Printed in the United States of America

iUniverse rev. date: 4/01/2010

For my family,

for sharing my camping experience

Contents

Introduction

THIS BOOK IS TARGETED at three types of people:

1. Those who already camp occasionally and enjoy it most of the time, but still find the preparation and packing grueling and time consuming, and dread the occasional mishap. They're looking for a way to simplify and improve the experience.
2. Those who have camped only a few times, but discontinued it for some reason. Perhaps they had one bad experience camping and just don't want to risk another similar experience, or are just unconvinced they can ever have a nice time camping.
3. Those who have never camped before but are willing to give it a try, either for the experience, economic reasons, or both, but just need a little coaching or encouragement.

I am also writing this book for myself. After many years of camping, including many great and a few not-so-great experiences, I feel compelled to share my experiences and what I learned so others can enjoy camping either more or more often.

I often discuss my camping trips with friends and relatives and I give a totally balanced account, telling them about the good things like family togetherness, the warmth of a campfire, or beautiful starry nights, as well as the challenges like rain, cold, bugs, etc. Most of the time after hearing my stories, they look somewhat envious and tell me they would like to go camping too, but then give me one or more reasons why they don't. After exhaustive non-scientific research, here are the top six reasons many people provide for not camping more often, or at all:

1. My spouse hates camping.
2. My spouse hates camping.
3. I don't know where to go.
4. It's too big a hassle getting ready and packing.
5. I don't have the necessary equipment and can't afford to buy it.

6. My spouse hates camping.

I won't take responsibility for selecting new spouses for these people, but I am confident I can help resolve some of the above issues and, hopefully, that will also resolve issues for the spouse.

Principles of this Book

This book is based on two principles that I think are necessary for camping to be not only tolerable, but enjoyable. The goal is not just to "survive" camping, but to enjoy it and want to do it again and again. These principles are:

- Camping must be Simple; and
- Camping must be Cheap

Let me explain what I mean by both of these.

Camping Must be Simple. By simple, I mean that every step, from planning the trip, preparing gear, packing, unpacking, and setting up and taking down camp should take very little preparation and time. I also mean simple in terms of keeping the whole experience flexible, unrushed, and uncomplicated. For example, a camping trip is usually not the time to rush around trying to squeeze as many activities, tours, shows, etc. into as little time as possible. If camping requires hours of planning, preparation, and packing, just to drive someplace for one or two nights, and then return and spend more time unpacking and recovering, it will quickly get tiring and unappealing.

Some camping trips do require a little more planning, but most trips don't need to be like mobilizing for a military deployment, but rather just taking thirty minutes to throw some gear in the car and take off. In fact, that is my definition of simple and my goal for a one or two-nighter— I expect to be able to pack up and leave within thirty minutes. Likewise, upon reaching the campground, I expect to be able to unpack and set up tents, make fires, etc. within thirty minutes. And when we return home, I expect to be able to unload and unpack in thirty minutes. Not surprisingly, you'll find that the more often you camp, the simpler and more efficient it becomes because you know where everything is, what to take, what to leave, and how to pack.

Camping Must be Cheap. You'll notice that I'm not afraid to say "cheap" instead of the more socially acceptable "inexpensive" or "great value". As I write this, the United States is suffering one of the worst recessions in memory; friends who used to eat out several times a week are now eating at home; those who used to take expensive vacations to tropical places are now staying home (staycations), or worse, just going to visit the in-laws. "Cheap" is in vogue again. Besides, if other authors can target their books at "idiots" and "dummies", I can certainly target mine at "cheapskates." However, I'm confident that once they try camping, they'll want to do it more regardless of their vacation budget.

I see camping as not only a fun activity, but as a way to save huge amounts of money on vacation, or to get more vacation out of the same amount of money. Most of us have more need for vacation than budget to pay for it, so we end up either making the mistake of going into debt to meet the vacation need or we shortchange our vacation to stay within budget. For example, we all probably know somebody (maybe it's ourselves) who took big vacations only to end up spending the next five years paying for them on expensive credit card debt. Or, conversely, to save money, maybe we used most of our vacation days staying home and watching reruns of Seinfield and The Simpsons or even overstaying our welcome at relatives. Camping is a way to satisfy that need for a real vacation and also pay the rent on time.

Don't get me wrong. My family and I enjoy nice hotels as much as anybody else and, given a choice, we will sometimes choose to sleep in a nice hotel bed over a sleeping bag in a tent. However, most of us don't have the money to do that and, if camping allows us to get out more and do more things, it's worth it. For some people, the low cost of camping makes possible longer or multiple vacations away from home in the same year. For other people, camping may determine if they can afford any vacation at all.

Tent Camping

I'm also defining simple and cheap as meaning tent camping. Sure, there are many other ways to "camp", in varying degrees of comfort and luxury. There are pop-up tent trailers, camper shells on pickup trucks, trailers, boats, motor homes, even log cabins. Those are all nice and I may even use some of them once in a while myself, but compared to tent camping, they all violate either the simple or cheap principle, or both, so I won't discuss them here, but if you're interested in those options, I'm sure there are plenty of other great resources out there.

Camping as a Means to an End

Although my family has fun camping, it often is not the main goal of our vacation, but rather a means to that end. Camping need not be your destination, but rather can be part of the journey and an affordable form of lodging while you're doing *other things*, allowing you to travel and enjoy activities you otherwise might not.

As for what you can do while camping, most people have a mindset that camping must always be combined with some outdoor, rustic activity, such as visiting national parks, hiking, biking, rafting, fishing, bird-watching, etc. They figure if they're not doing those kinds of activities, they don't have a reason to camp. Those are all great activities, but camping can also be combined with just about any activity that would be appropriate while staying in a hotel. For example, our family has camped out while visiting beaches, theme parks, Washington DC, big city attractions, cultural places, and even indoor best-dress activities like church conferences. So think outside the vacation box and begin to visualize that it can be part of almost any kind of vacation.

A Third Principle

I could probably add a third principle, which is that camping *can* and *should* be enjoyable. I'm not talking about getting so excited about camping that you sell your house and all your belongings and set up permanent camp at a state or national park campground. (Besides, I understand the rangers make you leave after a few weeks anyway.) But, rather you want to prepare your equipment (and your attitude) to have a good time while you're camping and, when you reflect on the trip later, feel like it was a pleasant and worthwhile experience and something you would like to do again. The goal of camping should not be just to survive the night and, upon rising in the morning, giving thanks that you're still alive. Surviving is important too, but your goal should be for your trip to be enjoyable *because*, and not *despite*, you were camping.

What you won't see in this book:
* Long lists or appendix of lists for campgrounds, destinations, recipes, Web sites, etc., other than some minimum equipment and sample meals. Tastes vary, prices change, places go in and out of operation, and most things can be found on the Internet.
* Criticism of people who don't like camping or insist on more luxurious camping with trailers, etc. See first rule above.

CHAPTER ONE
The Zen of Camping

WE LIVE IN A world of contradictions; we like controlling the elements and our environment to maximize our comfort and safety, constantly tweaking the thermostat of life in search of that elusive Goldilocks state of everything being "just right". However, something inside us also seeks variety, adventure, even occasional discomfort (think marathon runners). We don't want to venture too far away from the confines of our home or for very long, but most of us want to check out the fringes once in a while and, after trying it, realize that we neither died nor regretted the trip. In fact, we enjoyed it. Camping gets us out of our secure, regulated, artificially lit, temperature- and humidity-controlled, home environment and figuratively pushes us out of our comfort zone into the middle of a less-secure, less predictable, sensory experience. It can be a little scary, but something inside us seeks the adventure and the risk. The smell and feel of the fire, the intense blackness of night, the sounds of insects and wildlife in the trees and brush, the heightened taste and smell of the food, the feeling of the unfamiliar climate on our skins. It's a sensory feast that, let's face it, we can't really experience at home or in a hotel very easily, if at all. Dare I say, a night camping can actually be a transcendent or spiritual experience?

The Campfire
I've heard all sorts of theories about why we enjoy sitting around and staring into a fire, also known as fire-gazing. Is it our primitive hunter-gatherer

DNA coming to the surface? When we sit in our recliner at home with the remote firmly in hand, staring at the TV for hours on end, is that, in fact, our conscious or subconscious attempt to create the primitive fire-gazing experience? We may also light fires in the fireplace, sit around fire rings on the patio, or even play a DVD of a fireplace or campfire on our TV's. I don't know the real reason we're drawn to the warmth and beauty of a campfire, except that it's … well, warm and beautiful.

The Night

Verlyn Klinkenborgand, in a November 2008 article in National Geographic, discusses how humans don't instinctively seek out the dark; in fact, we have "engineered it to receive us by filling it with light". But the unintended consequence in most of our cities is "light pollution", which not only disrupts wildlife, but makes it increasingly difficult for humans to escape the constant glare of artificial light.

Klinkenborgand explains how, while we may not realize it, we need darkness just like we need light. As we continue to extend the day and shorten the night, we "short-circuit" the body's sensitive response to light, disrupting our own sleep-wake cycles.

Complete darkness has become so foreign to us that when we happen to experience it, it can actually be unnerving, even frightening. If you've ever been on a guided tour of cave, at some point the guide probably turned off the light to demonstrate just how dark total darkness can be. I remember being on one of these tours and when the lights went out, even for just thirty seconds or so, people were noticeably uncomfortable and anxious to turn the lights back on.

In some remote areas as well, after sunset and away from city lights, you notice that it gets really, really dark—darker than you ever thought possible. The complete darkness makes you respect it and reminds you that, if only temporarily, it's in charge and it's not going to wait for you to finish dinner or pitch the tent. It's pushing you headfirst into a simpler lifestyle, similar to a hundred years ago before electricity, when sunrise and sunset dictated your activities and darkness could not be manipulated or bent to your ever-ambitious schedule. This shortening of the day can be unnerving for some people, who are used to staying active and keeping their environment illuminated into the late hours.

And yet, the night can be a special experience while camping. It doesn't necessarily mean you have to go to bed at sunset (although that's an option), but it limits your activities and, like it or not, makes you slow down and relax.

Except for the few people who live in rural areas, camping is one of the few opportunities for us to get away from the city lights and experience real darkness. No houselights, traffic lights, streetlights, nightlights, blinking clock radios, etc. Just pure, raw, unfiltered darkness.

The increased glare of city lights also directly affects our enjoyment of the night sky. As the ambient light around our populated areas increases, the visibility of stars and planets decreases. This fading of stars in the sky has happened gradually, almost imperceptibly, so that we barely notice what we don't notice anymore. Camping allows us, in most places, to get away from the light of the populated areas and experience true nighttime and, on a clear night, a beautiful star-filled sky.

Unplugged
Similar to the way the darkness forces us to simplify our evening activities, camping in most places offers us the opportunity to experience life "unplugged", or at least less plugged in. Sure, no matter how back-to-nature we plan to be, we'll probably still have our cell phones, and desperate people can usually find a plug outlet somewhere, but I strongly recommend you leave all other communication and entertainment devices home. A few days unplugged will not only contribute to that simpler, more relaxing time mentioned above, but will also, in its own devious way, encourage you to find more interactive, sociable ways to spend time with your loved ones.

The Beauty of Imperfection
Camping and nature have a certain imperfect messiness and asymmetry to them that appeals to us as we try to escape the monotony of our daily clean, neat, orderly lives. It's like the preference of real grass on a football field, with its grassy smell, bare patches, uneven texture, and holes, over the smooth, uniform surface of artificial turf; like a real Christmas tree with its natural scent, asymmetrical shape and gaps, and transitory needles over the uniform tidiness of an artificial tree; like a painting, with its less-than-precise lines and colors over the optical accuracy of a photograph; or like a homemade cookie with its irregular shape and color to the assembly-line store-bought variety. Your campsite probably won't have boundary lines, fences, or any other kind of definition, but instead just a fuzzy, ambiguous line separating you from others or the woods. You'll have no locks or Do Not Disturb signs.

You're neither alone nor in company with others. With no thermostats, you'll experience all the irregularities of temperature. In camping, asymmetry and imperfection are the rule and remind us that we're dealing with real, genuine things.

Nature as Therapy

Like many of these activities, camping is not the only way to experience nature, but it has a way of creating more opportunities to do so than just about anything else. Anyone who has spent much time camping or hiking will attest that time in the outdoors and in nature can have a therapeutic effect on us. They are usually not sure why or how to explain it, but they know it carries such benefits as increased relaxation and concentration, positive attitude, improved health, gratitude, tolerance, and new perspectives.

Conversely, if exposure to nature provides these kinds of benefits, does it also hold true that lack of exposure to nature can actually harm us? Many of us have grandparents or great grandparents who were farmers, but with each generation, as people migrate to the urban centers, we become farther removed from the land and nature. Fifty or a hundred years ago, nature was all around us, unavoidable. Now, without an active, determined effort to experience it, we can easily go months or even years without direct exposure to nature.

In his 2005 book *Last Child in the Woods*, Richard Louv coined the term *nature-deficit disorder* as the negative consequences of not getting enough exposure to natural environments. While emphasizing that it's not a formal diagnosable medical condition, he cites symptoms like diminished use of the senses, attention difficulties, and higher rates of physical and emotional illness. Since the book's publication, a number of movements and initiatives have sprung up at the state and regional levels to address the need for more hands-on environmental education and contact with nature, most notably the *No Child Left Inside* campaign.

Louv recalls a fourth-grader in San Diego who said "I like to play indoors better, 'cause that's where all the electrical outlets are." Among some of his other observations:

- Direct or primary sensory experience with nature is being replaced by the vicarious, experience of television and other electronic media.
- Inventiveness and imagination of creative people are rooted in their early experiences in nature.

- Organized sports are not a legitimate substitute for unstructured, outdoor play.
- Direct exposure to nature is essential for physical and emotional health and symptoms of childhood mental disorders are intensified by children's disconnection from nature.
- Similarly, exposure to nature may be useful as a therapy for many maladies, similar to the demonstrated benefits of pet therapy, and can be used with or, when appropriate, even replacing medications or behavioral therapies. For example, University of Illinois researchers Andrea Faber Taylor, Frances Kuo, and William C. Sullivan have found that green outdoor spaces relieve the symptoms of attention-deficit disorders. By comparison, activities indoors, such as watching TV, or outdoors in paved, non-green areas, increase these children's symptoms.
- People with disabilities gain enhanced body image and positive behavior changes from their camp experiences in nature.
- Nature also has a spiritual dimension for us and many transcendent childhood experiences happen in nature where children can easily contemplate infinity and eternity.
- The most effective way to connect children to nature is for parents to connect themselves to nature and see time in nature not as leisure time, but rather as an essential investment in their children's health.

CHAPTER TWO
Camping versus Hotel Lodging

WHEN CONSIDERING A CAMPING trip, the alternative for most people is traditional hotel lodging, so let's take a look at the pros and cons of camping compared with hotels. You may be surprised. Again, keep in mind our principles of Simple and Cheap.

Camping is More Affordable
This is, of course, stating the obvious, and will often be the primary reason people choose to camp instead of staying at a hotel. But just for dramatic effect, let's compare the costs for a family of four for five nights of camping versus hotel, as illustrated on the accompanying table.

- Hotel – Rates vary dramatically by geography, popularity of location, and class of hotel, but at a minimum, a night of lodging for one room will run close to $100. Fancier hotels in resort areas can be over $300 a night, but for ease of math, let's just use $100 per night. But wait, that's not all. If you stay at a hotel, unless it has kitchen facilities (which will increase the cost of the room), you'll need to eat out for most of your meals. Even fast food for every meal will end up costing you at least another $50 per day, but realistically, closer to $100 or more. Total for five nights of lodging and food: approximately $1,000.

- Tent Camping – Again, rates may vary by geography, popularity of location, or class of campground, but here are some rough guidelines based on a typical state park campground with shower facilities. At most state parks, a single campsite will run about $10–$20 per night (per site, not per person) and usually allows up to two tents, plenty big enough for our hypothetical family of four. Some parks may also charge a daily admission fee to the park of $8–$10 (per car), less for state residents. An annual state park pass may also be available and ends up being less expensive than the daily pass if you stay in parks within the same state for more than three or four days during the year. For meals, let's assume you cook two meals a day at the campsite and "splurge" at a restaurant for one meal a day. Total meal cost could end up as much as $40 per day. Total for five nights of camping and food: approximately $350.

	Camping	Hotel
Hotel Lodging	$0	$500
Park Fees	50	0
Campsite Fees	100	0
Food/Meals	200	500
Total	$350	$1,000

A savings of $650 for five nights! For many people, those savings can be the difference between going on vacation and staying home. Of course, I've excluded the cost of purchasing camping equipment, which I'll cover later, but most people already have invested in most of the gear they'll need and generally all it takes is one camping trip for the savings to recoup the cost of all your equipment.

Intentional Education

Most national and state parks have ranger programs and nature walks and they're usually free of charge. Many of these will be listed at the park Web site, allowing you to schedule and plan your trip around them (but you may not want to tell your kids this – see below). You can also indulge your interests in geology, caves, archeology, geography, etc. Hotel lodging may also give you access to some activities, but camping puts you right there in the middle of the action and makes it easier to access.

Accidental Education

Now what do I mean by this? Have you ever visited somewhere or had an experience that, when looking back, you realized you learned a lot that was never part of the original agenda? The natural spontaneity and unpredictable nature of camping means you are guaranteed to see, hear, smell, taste, touch, or otherwise experience something you hadn't even thought of when you first planned your trip. This is particularly true for kids, who often respond much better to accidental education than the more deliberate types. In fact, for most kids, I recommend NOT telling them about any potential educational experiences they may have on the trip. They may turn and run the other way! Instead, just tell them they'll have fun. You can just keep to yourself the fact that they'll end up absorbing all sorts of interesting and educational things.

In our experience, we've had accidental education in things like cooking and preparing food, emergency preparedness, nature and wildlife, geology, archaeology, etc. On several trips through volcanic regions, we stopped at ranger stations and visitor centers and learned a lot about volcanoes. On camping trips in state parks built around old iron ghost towns, we learned about the people, homes, industry, and culture that used to be there. In a camping trip to Yellowstone National Park, we arrived at Old Faithful just in time to see the president of the United States visiting with his family. My kids were able to shake hands with the president – something totally spontaneous and unpredictable that we would have missed had we arrived thirty minutes earlier or later. On a walk near our campground on South Manitou Island in Lake Michigan, my kids and I received an unscheduled lesson in predator-prey relationships as we stumbled upon a snake attempting to swallow a very large toad. Cool. Could you and your family have these same kinds of experiences while staying in a hotel? It's possible, but the flexible nature of camping and the increased proximity to natural environments increases the odds you'll have these kinds of experiences while camping.

Fresh, Cheap, Delicious Food in a Campfire Atmosphere
Nothing more to say here.

Open Space
Maybe not as important to adults as to kids, but camping offers the open space that little kids need to get the "wiggles" out. A hotel room may offer 400–500 square feet of space for kids to play around. A campsite, by extension into the whole park, offers acres and acres.

Access to Beauty Away from Crowds
Camping makes accessible many beautiful, fascinating, and uncrowded places that otherwise could only be seen on postcards. For example, some of the most beautiful areas belonging to state and national parks are only accessible to the people willing to drive several miles on an old dirt road or even hike several

miles and camp in the backcountry. The nearest hotel might be many miles away, but camping can put you right in the midst of the beauty. That little extra bit of effort to get there means ninety percent of everybody else won't bother to make the trip and tends to keep the area uncrowded and unspoiled. Several years ago, I took my three sons on a camping trip to South Manitou Island in Lake Michigan. It was not what I would call primitive, rough camping by any means, but to get there, we had to take a forty-five-minute ferry ride to the island and then backpack one mile to our campsite. We spent several days walking the beaches and seeing all the unspoiled nature the island had to offer, but saw very few other people.

Family Time
More than almost any other activity, camping has a way of encouraging closeness and communication among family members. Upon check-in to a hotel, the typical family, even though they are in close physical quarters, may often retreat socially to the same distractions or entertainment they had at home – the TV, surfing the Internet, online social networking, or playing computer games. These are all fun activities, but are usually passive, done in isolation, and don't encourage a lot of family communication or togetherness. At a campsite, assuming you leave these things home (I hope you do), I've found that the family gets more engaged with each other – we have to work together to set up camp, build a fire, and make meals, which encourages participation, cooperation, and communication. It helps explain, I think, why families fifty or a hundred years ago were probably closer and communicated more. They spent a lot more time working together either on the farm or around the house and had few other alternatives or distractions. Admit it, it's easier just to veg out in the hotel room and let your kids be zombies in front of the TV. Getting your family engaged and communicating can require work and persistence to overcome all the other distractions available. Camping simply removes most of those distractions, and communication and togetherness rush in to fill the void.

Pets are Welcome
Most hotels either don't allow pets or will charge an extra fee for them. Most campgrounds, on the other hand welcome pets without any fees. The only requirements are the same as you'll encounter anywhere else: they must be leashed and well-behaved. And, by the way, pets love camping.

Camping is More Social
Imagine checking into a hotel for vacation and, within an hour of check-in, you've met the people in all the rooms near you, your kids are playing

together, and you've perhaps scheduled a card game with some of them for later in the evening. Doesn't happen does it? It may not even happen back home with neighbors you've lived next to for ten years. Just as camping encourages socializing among immediate family members, it also encourages that behavior among your campsite neighbors, even if they were complete strangers an hour earlier. Something about the absence of walls and other barriers brings people together who otherwise would never meet.

Camping is More Memorable

I don't mean this as much from a sentimental perspective as from our literal ability to remember and recall memories from vacations that involve camping more than those involving hotel lodging. Educators often remind us that the more senses we use to experience or learn something, the more likely we are to retain the knowledge. This is just my theory, but I believe that camping, with its heightened exposure to weather, sights, sounds, smells, and tastes, engages all the senses much more directly than hotel lodging. I know this is true in my case when I reflect on vacations throughout my life. The experiences I recall in the most vivid detail are the camping trips.

Downsides of Camping

This wouldn't be a balanced portrayal of camping without acknowledging some of the more challenging aspects.

- Packing/unpacking and logistics. Because you're taking your lodging and kitchen with you, camping generally will require more packing and unpacking than hotel lodging, and the more places you camp during your trip, the more you have to set up and break camp. This gets easier each time you do it, but it can still be tedious. Also, a hotel allows you to arrive at the last minute and immediately start some other activity, such as going out for dinner, or if very late, just go to bed. Likewise, you can wake up, check out, and be on the road first thing in the morning. Camping, on the other hand, requires a minimum amount of set up and unpacking after arrival, and take-down and packing before departing. For these reasons, when camping, you'll usually want to arrive before dark to start meal preparation or get a fire going, and to avoid having to set up a tent in the dark. If you've got a busy checklist of things to do, hotel lodging, therefore, may actually allow you to fit more activities into your day.

- Reservations. Hotels usually won't charge you for a reservation and will hold it until late at night. Most, but not all, campgrounds will take reservations, usually for a fee, but may have a deadline after which you lose it.
- Uncertainty. Face it, camping may have a degree of a stress or anxiety because your enjoyment is highly subject to things you can't control: the weather, neighbors, bugs, etc. Some hard-core campers may tell you that they had a great time even though it rained every day; or, they may say the uncertainty of things like that make it more of an adventure. But for most of the rest of us, the even-slight chance of something like several days of bad weather during a vacation that is primarily outdoors can cause some anxiety.
- Children may require more attention. This can be good or bad depending on the goals of your vacation, but the lack of other distractions can leave some kids puzzled about what to do and you'll need to step in and get them engaged in helping do camp chores or go exploring in the woods.
- Lower quality sleep. I haven't met very many people who get a better night's sleep camping than at home (or in hotel), and I've met many people who get a worse sleep. There are some ways to alleviate some of the problem, but campers generally just accept the fact that they will not sleep as well.
- The grunge factor. After a few nights of camping, some people start to weary of the dirt, grime, damp clothing, and extra effort it takes to stay clean and dry. I'm not saying it's not possible to stay clean and dry, but it does take extra effort. For this and other reasons mentioned earlier, I don't recommend camping trips in excess of four or five nights. You can have too much of a good thing.

CHAPTER THREE
Planning and Budgeting Your Trip

WE THOUGHT WE WERE all ready for a camping trip. The plan was to pack up quickly and leave Friday evening after work, drive a few hours to a nice location, set up camp before sunset, make a fire, eat, and relax, and then return home the next day to tell our friends what a great, relaxing, family-bonding time we had. However, the last part never really happened. First of all, we spent hours locating gear and packing up the car, which got us on the road much later than planned. Then we realized it was farther than we thought, and we got lost and it took several hours to reach the campground, only to arrive so late it was lacking a selection of good campsites. By then we had to set up camp in the dark while beginning to get hungry, at which time we realized we had forgotten matches or bug spray or tent stakes or the rain fly or some of the food or (you fill in the blank). By the time the fire was started, it was 10:00 PM and we were really hungry and stressed out. We no longer had the patience to cook a meal and ended up eating cheese and crackers from a nearby convenience store and just going to bed. Then we had to leave early the next morning to get home in time for other commitments. The end result of a trip like that is that it was rushed and not at all relaxing, and if this had happened to us on our first or second time camping, it just might have discouraged us from going camping again … ever.

Fortunately, we had camped enough to know that it can really be a pleasant experience, if planned right. Planning and budgeting your trip, or the "Where and How Long" of camping, is one of the most important steps in having a successful camping trip. The goal is to make camping easy and comfortable, yet flexible and spontaneous enough that you're not locked into a rigid schedule.

How Long to Camp
- One-nighters. These are easy to fit in without a lot of trip planning as long as they hold to the principle of keeping it simple. If it takes you longer than twenty minutes to load the car and be on your way, you'll quickly get discouraged from going through all the packing and preparation just for one night of camping. Also, keep your one-nighter destination less than two hours away; anything more than that starts to feel too rushed just for one night, as the above example illustrates.
- Two-plus-nighters. If the destination is more than two hours away, I recommend going for at least two nights and then spending at least two nights in any single spot. This will reduce the rush, allow you to take advantage of planning and packing only once, and make it a much more relaxing trip. Even as you extend your trips to three nights or a week or more and want to visit multiple attractions during the same trip, I've found that it's less stressful and more relaxing to stay at least two nights in any one location, using each site as a base camp to visit nearby attractions. This approach may mean you drive a little farther from your base camp to the attractions, but it pays off in reduced time and complexity of taking down and setting up camp additional times. Remember, the goal is a simple, relaxing trip, not the logistical camping equivalent of the Iraq War meets Orlando, Florida.

Where to Go
The duration of the trip will likely influence where you go as well, and this is limited only by your imagination. Sometimes just camping is the destination, without any concrete plans to see or do something else. But often, camping is the means to an end, or a way to make seeing or doing something else more fun and affordable. Would you describe yourself as more of a "national park" person or an "amusement park" person? The former is usually more compatible with camping, but that doesn't mean you can't camp while visiting amusement or theme parks, or even popular cities too. For example, I took my family to see Washington DC and we camped every night in a beautiful state park in Virginia, about an hour south of DC. We spent the days visiting historical sites and the evenings at camp. We got the best of both worlds.

Another example demonstrating that there needn't be any limit to when or where you go camping was our honeymoon. Before you roll your eyes about somebody actually going camping on his honeymoon, hear me out. My wife and I were struggling college students (are there any other kind?) when we got married. We were also raised in very practical homes that didn't have a lot of money to spend and avoided debt like the plague. So when it came time to plan our honeymoon, we were left with the choices of going nowhere or taking a low-cost driving vacation to the Northwest. We realized that the less we spent on lodging, the more days we could spend on our honeymoon, so we settled on one night in the historic Empress Hotel in Victoria, Vancouver Island, Canada, combined with four or five nights of camping at scenic areas along the way. It turned out to be a great honeymoon with wonderful memories, with a mixture of European-style glamour in Victoria and beautiful nature in the national forests of Washington.

So, first decide what you want to see and do—the destination or destinations of your trip. Then look for campgrounds near or along the way. America is a very camp-friendly country and I would estimate that there is a public campground or wilderness area that allows camping within an hour's drive of just about every person in America. Here are some of the more popular choices for where to camp.

- Private campgrounds. These cover a wide range in terms of quality. Some are in remote, beautiful areas and others appear to be in somebody's backyard next to their clothesline. Some have every amenity, including showers, swimming pools, and recreation halls, while others have only very basic services. Because many cater heavily to RV's or other modern forms of camping with electrical hookups, I've had a hard time finding private campgrounds that are appropriate for tent campers, so I generally avoid them unless they're the only option in the area.
- State Parks. In my experience, these are some of the best values and most accessible in the country. You may not be near a national park, but almost everyone is within an hour or two of a state park with camping facilities. State parks quite often have conveniences like showers and flush toilets and fees are usually very affordable, as low as $10 per night, including showers, and a little more for electricity hookups.
- National Parks, Forests, and Lakeshores. These are less numerous or accessible than state parks, and those in remote areas often

don't offer as many conveniences like showers or flush toilets, but they have the advantage of usually offering a lot of natural beauty or sites of historical significance. They're also usually very affordable, with fees similar to state parks.

The Itinerary

The word "itinerary" conjures up dreaded images of detailed and immaculously organized multi-destination trips or cruises, but in this context it simply means putting together a rough sketch of what you'll do when. One of the advantages of camping road trips is you can be more flexible and spontaneous and totally change your itinerary in the middle of a trip if it suits your needs, in most cases without cancellation fees or other extra costs.

I recommend keeping the pace relaxed. For multi-day trips, avoid traveling more than five or six hours per day. When transferring from one site to another, you want to break camp and get to your next campground by early afternoon so you'll have a better selection of sites and plenty of time to set up camp again. Most campgrounds accept reservations, usually for an additional fee, and you may want to do this if it's a very popular place or if you expect to arrive late in the evening, but generally you'll want to plan your trip to arrive early enough that reservations are not necessary, and you can maintain the flexibility to change your plans at the last minute. Do your best to allow for spontaneity.

My experience of over planning: We were living in Japan and decided to go on a one-week camping trip to a volcanic area on the southern island of Kyushu. By the way, contrary to most images of Japan, there is actually much open land in the countryside with many nice campgrounds and parks, and many Japanese love to camp. The extremely high cost of traditional lodging also makes camping in Japan one of the few affordable ways to travel there. Worried about crowds, we had made advance reservations (and paid all the fees) at various campgrounds for every night of our trip. About halfway into our trip, while enjoying the beautiful sights at Mount Aso, we realized not only that we wanted to stay in the Aso area a little longer, but there was no way we would be able to travel to the next campground and check in before their 6:00 PM deadline. We worried we would not be able to find another campground nearby with any vacancies and that we may end up sleeping in the car in a parking lot somewhere. We started driving down the mountain and ended up taking what we thought was a shortcut to the highway. It turned out, instead, to lead us to a beautiful hot spring resort at the foot of the mountain that included some limited campsites. It was like stumbling into

Shangri-la and we decided to stay two nights and enjoy bathing in the hot springs. We loved the place so much that we went back again in the middle of the winter. What started as a problem of over planning fortunately had a good ending. We learned that, for future trips, it's best to keep some flexibility and not make reservations for every night.

Spontaneity and Flexibility

Campgrounds in popular areas fill up just like hotels and sometimes it's necessary to reserve in advance, but I recommend keeping the schedule as flexible as possible, allowing you room to adjust and modify as needed. Our family recently planned a camping trip that would circumnavigate Lake Michigan, stopping and camping at at least four different campgrounds in ten days. Heading north from Chicago, our first stop was at Peninsula State Park in Door County, Wisconsin. We were so impressed with the beauty and range of activities there that we ended up spending the entire trip there.

Another example of the excitement of spontaneity while camping: My family and I were on a week-long camping trip in the Upper Peninsula of Michigan. We had visited some interesting sites of natural beauty before driving all the way west to Copper Harbor on the shores of Lake Superior only to be met with a miserable, cold rain storm, which is typical of the unpredictable weather in that part of the state. After one night there in the rain, we decided to surrender to the weather, abort the "mission", and make a marathon drive southeast back toward home. On the way back along the north shore of Lake Michigan, the weather suddenly cleared up again just as we saw a sign for Fayette State Park. We had read nothing about this place, had no plans to visit it, but needed a break and pulled over. We were pleasantly surprised to find the ruins of a historic nineteenth-century ironworks town right on the shores of Lake Michigan, and in the midst of restoration by the park service. Even better, we seemed to have the whole place almost to ourselves. We ended up camping in a beautiful pine-covered area and spending the whole next day walking and exploring the sites. It was totally unplanned, but ended up being one of the highlights of our trip.

Plan B

Considering that camping is primarily an outdoor activity, subject to weather and other uncertainties, you should always include a "Plan B" in your trip planning. If you experience unexpected rain, for example, you can still stay dry in your tent at night while sleeping—for at least a few nights—but the activities you planned for the daytime hours may no longer seem practical.

For example, if your good weather Plan A was to go to the beach or go for a hike, your bad weather Plan B could include one or more of the following:

- If you're in a state or national park, it's very likely they'll have a nature center of some kind.
- Some parks and recreation areas also offer arts and craft classes.
- If you're in an area of historical significance, go visit a local museum or tour historic buildings.
- If you're near the ocean or the Great Lakes, visit local lighthouses.
- Do some geocaching or earthcaching by car.
- Visit and walk around the nearest town. The rural areas where you find many of the state and national parks often include small, historic, picturesque towns with interesting locally-owned shops and merchandise. Patronize these local merchants, strike up a conversation, learn a little about the area, and you may find yourself reminiscing later that that was the most memorable part of the trip.
- Satisfy the urge for water sports by finding the nearest indoor pool or water park.
- Visit an arcade or bowling alley.
- If you're really, really desperate, hit the local shopping mall for a few hours.

Equipment Check and Trial Camping
A week or several days before leaving on your camping trip, you should go through all your equipment and make sure it's complete and ready. If you need to purchase any items, it's usually cheaper to do it in familiar stores near home than in rural areas. If it's been several months or more since your last camping trip, going through the following checklist will help ensure a camping trip with few unpleasant surprises:

- Set up the tent and make sure no parts are missing or broken. On your trip, you may be required to set up a tent in the dark, or in the rain or wind, and that's not the time to start reading the instructions or figuring out which pole goes where.
- Assemble and fire up your camp stove and make sure you have the correct fuel.
- Check your camping box and other supplies for completeness.

- Check out the availability and quality of your sleeping bags. If it's been a while since you last used them, you may find mold or other problems and need to get them dry-cleaned.

Finally, and this may seem a little silly, but if you have never been camping before, or if it's been over a year, I recommend doing a trial campout, or dress rehearsal, before your first trip. If you have a yard, simply pitch a tent and spend a night in the backyard. If you don't have a yard, you could try it in a garage or even an open room in the house. Just one night will introduce you to the feeling of sleeping on the ground and help give you an idea of any special limitations or discomfort you have so you can plan for them on the real trip. For example, you may find that your sleeping bag is not as warm as you thought or that your back needs extra padding on the ground.

CHAPTER FOUR
Equipment and Packing

For equipment, let's start with the basics or bare essentials of equipment. I break the basics into two categories. The Basics-I include the absolute minimum to get you through the night. Think about it: if necessary, you can improvise just about every other part of the camping trip without spending much money or missing out on the fun, but at a minimum you need a way to comfortably and affordably sleep through the night. This is also the part that will end up saving you the most money compared with traditional vacations because hotel lodging is usually the most expensive part of a vacation.

The Basics-I: Getting Through the Night
- Ground Cloth
- Tent
- Sleeping Bags and Sleeping Pads
- Clothes
- Hat or Cap
- Rain Jacket or Poncho
- Personal Hygiene/Grooming (soap, toothbrush, etc.)
- Towel
- Camera
- Day Pack
- Water Bottle
- Baby/Toddler Backpack (if you have very small children)
- First Aid Kit
- Bug Spray

- Sunscreen
- Pocketknife
- Flashlight
- Matches/Lighter
- Newspaper
- Tissue
- Hatchet or Saw

After the Basics-I to get through the night, you'll want to focus on equipment to cook and eat meals. After lodging, cooking your own meals is the next area that will save you the most money compared with eating in restaurants during traditional vacations. I call these supplies, plus a few miscellaneous items, the Basics-II.

The Basics-II: Cooking, Eating, and Miscellaneous
- Stove and Fuel
- Food for one or two days
- Water (if not available in the campground)
- Camping Box, which includes:
    - Large Saucepan and Lid
    - Small Saucepan and Lid
    - Frypan or Griddle
    - Paper Towels
    - Ziploc Bags
    - Aluminum Foil
    - Large Spoon
    - Kabob Sticks/Weenie Sticks
    - Vegetable Oil
    - Dish Soap
    - Sanitary Wipes or Hand Sanitizer
    - Sponge/Pad
    - Dish Towel
    - Pencil/Paper
    - Salt & Pepper
    - Extra Matches/Lighter
    - Tongs
    - Spatula/Turner
    - Can Opener (or pocketknife)
    - Kitchen Knife
    - Potato Peeler
    - Cutting Board

- Utensils
- Cups
- Bowls
- Plates
- Garbage Bag
- Duct Tape
- Bungee Cord
- Fishing Line
- Safety Pins and Needle/Thread
- Rope
- Collapsible Grill
- Hot Pad
- Pitcher/Water Container

A few words about the importance of the camping box: I used to spend hours making lists, searching for things, and packing gear each time our family went on a campout, and then still worrying all the way to the campground if maybe I forgot something. To avoid this "packing anxiety" I came up with the camping box after seeing how well the similar "patrol box" concept worked in the Boy Scouts. The idea is that you want all essential cooking supplies and a few other items in one organized, easy-to-find place, like a box. Gather all the supplies you need just once, put them in the box, and avoid using them for anything else between camping trips. This will help you avoid having to repack these items every time you take a camping trip. What could otherwise take several hours of searching and packing becomes a few minutes. Just remember to pack the box before you leave and your packing anxiety is relieved. You'll notice that most of the above items in the camping box are either very cheap to acquire or are already available around the house, often in duplicate, and seldom used. I recommend, therefore, collecting these items, donating them to the camping box, and then use them for NOTHING else. You can use a cardboard box or, even better, a rubber or plastic tote container. You'll also appreciate this during your camping trip because it will make it faster and easier to pack up and move to the next campground.

Camping box

Next, again in order of priority and if there is still space in the car, let's move onto optional items that are for additional comfort. These are all "nice to have" and, personally, I do my best to find room for some of these things, like the air mattress; but if you run out of space, they can be left behind without detracting too much from a positive camping experience.

Comfort and Convenience (space permitting)
- Air Mattress
- Cots
- Lawn Chairs
- Portable playpen (for crawling babies)
- Camp Cookers/Pie Irons
- Dutch Oven
- Cooler and ice
- Card games and small sports equipment
- Reading Material

That's it. Even if you still have a little corner of space left in your vehicle, I recommend not taking any more items because it just adds to the time and complexity of preparation and packing/unpacking. Save that space for souvenirs. You might think some things are missing here that many people consider absolutely necessary, like strollers, playpens, lawn chairs, dining tents, toys, stereos, tables, heaters, fans, DVD players, charcoal or gas grilles, coffee pots, large games, or sports equipment. But think about it, none of these things are really necessary to get through the night or enjoy a campfire, and they just take up more space. I'm not saying don't ever bring these items, but rather pack the basics first, then cooking supplies, then comfort items (as space allows), and then, if you still have space, consider taking them, but realizing that it may not be worth the trouble.

Family-size dome tent

Acquiring Equipment

There are many misperceptions about the cost of acquiring the equipment to start camping. Some people think they can't camp without making a shopping expedition to an expensive, premium brand outdoor store, buying $600 tents, $300 sleeping bags, $100 sleeping pads, $10 water bottles, fancy cookware, and all the other expensive gadgets. Of course this would violate the cheap principle and is totally unnecessary.

Hard-core survivalist types might go to the other extreme and recommend that you buy next to nothing, make your own, or do without. Indeed, there are handbooks out there, like the Boy Scout Fieldbook and others, which actually show you how to make homemade sleeping bags, tents, snow boots, cookware, etc. They're great ideas, but contrary to the Simple principle of this book, so I don't recommend it except for the craftsman or hobbyist.

Instead, I recommend a compromise between these two extremes, using as many things as possible around the house and purchasing any remaining essentials from discount stores locally or online.

Let's start with outfitting the Basics-I. If you're like most people, you already have a tarp or ground cloth, tent, and several sleeping bags in the house. You probably bought them for a camping trip, used them once, maybe twice, and then put them away forever. Well, pull them out of the closet and start using them again! If you need to acquire even the basics, here's what you can expect:

- Tarp/ground cloth. You need at least one for each tent and the size should be at least as big as the floor of the tent. If it's a little larger than the tent floor, you can use part of the tarp as a mudroom area for your tent. Since tarps take up very little packing room, I recommend taking an extra one or two just for things like having picnics on the ground, giving the dog a place to lie away from the dirt, emergency kitchen rain fly, etc.
- Tents. You can pick up decent three-person dome tents for $40 and surprisingly good six-person dome tents for about $100. For a little more money, you can even get tents with multiple rooms or compartments, allowing you to have separate rooms for your kids, your dog, and your mother-in-law (not necessarily in that order). Some also all mudroom areas, all sorts of storage compartments, built-in pet doors, and other nice features. Pay special attention to the rain fly, making sure it is big enough and designed to keep rain off all sides of the tent. The rain fly should be separate and not permanently attached to the main tent, allowing you to leave it off for better ventilation during hot, dry weather.
- Sleeping bags. Prices run a wide range from $30 to $300 or more, but you should be able to buy decent, general-use 32-degree (0 Celsius) bags for under $50 each and this is usually adequate for most casual campers. If you plan to backpack or camp in colder temperatures, you can get light-weight or reasonably good zero-degree (-18 Celsius) bags for under $100. Generally, you have to make tradeoffs among comfort, size, weight, and temperature rating. The general-use large, fluffy rectangular bags, made of

either natural or synthetic fibers, are usually very comfortable, and allow room to spread out more while sleeping. However, they can also be bulky and heavy and take up a lot of packing space; also, they are not appropriate for backpacking and may not have a very low temperature rating. Most lighter-weight and cold weather "mummy" bags, on the other hand, are often made of high-tech synthetic fibers (or the more expensive goose down), and are more compact and better for backpacking or off-season camping; but they also provide a much snugger sleep area. A word about sleeping bag temperature ratings: everybody's cold tolerance is a little different and ratings are not consistent, so play it safe and buy a bag rated 10–20 degrees lower than the lowest temperatures you are expecting.

- Sleeping pads. Amazingly, some sleeping pads, such as the ultra-light, self-inflating type, cost more than sleeping bags, but you should be able to find adequate pads starting at about $10 each.
- Day Packs. These can be as simple as what the kids use for school.
- Baby/Toddler Backpack. If you have very young children, this can be a lifesaver and is well worth taking—instead of, not in addition to—a stroller. Strollers have their place in society, such as department stores, shopping malls, sidewalks, and other flat, smooth surfaces. But they are usually not appropriate for camping trips, where they're too bulky to pack, don't leave your hands free, and, unless they're the really expensive kind with large wheels, not very useful on dirt or rocky trails. Baby backpacks, on the other hand, keep your hands free and give you much more flexibility in where you go and how you spend the day. We have also found that infants are much more content and quiet while riding in a backpack than in a stroller; I suspect this is because they enjoy the elevated view and also feel more secure leaning against the parent. Sure, baby backpacks add some weight and are not recommended for people with back problems, but are a great way to handle kids on your trip. Prices start around $75.
- First Aid Kit. This is on the Basics-I list for good reason. Don't skimp or leave this home no matter how short your trip or how desperate you are for packing space. A simple kit that will prepare you for most emergencies shouldn't take up more space that a quart-size Ziploc bag. You can purchase excellent kits, but I actually recommend creating your own kit from supplies around

the house and keeping them in a small bathroom bag or Ziploc bag. That way, you get the brands and types of supplies that you know and prefer. Minimum recommended contents for your kit include: adhesive bandages in various sizes, sterile gauze pads, tape, antiseptic, antibiotic ointment, anti-itch or bug bite spray, scissors, tweezers, pain reliever, cold and allergy medicine, latex gloves, safety pins, and alcohol sterile wipes. Depending on how much personal first aid training you have, you might also want to pack a small manual or guidebook on basic first aid. Again, you can add more, but don't try to prepare for every possible emergency! Remember, be prepared, but keep it simple.

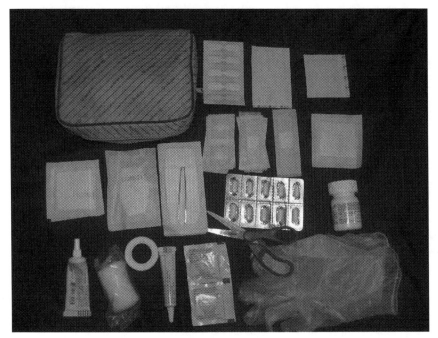

Basic first aid kit

There, even if you had to start completely from scratch, for about the cost of one or two nights in a nice hotel, you've outfitted a family of four with the basics to sleep through many nights year after year. **You have recouped your whole investment in just a couple nights of camping**! And, in a *week* of camping, your savings could be more than double; meaning, in business terms, you achieved a one hundred percent return on your investment in a week. Or, to put it another way, if you bought all your equipment and used it for just one week of camping and then threw it all in the trash, you would still come out way ahead financially. But in fact, most equipment will last for years; our tent and other gear have been used for over fourteen years in all kinds of weather and conditions, and should last many more. How well did your other investments do last year?

As for the Basics-II cooking and other supplies:
- Camp Stove. A two-burner stove is adequate for a group of four and can be purchased starting at about $40.
- Camping Box. You don't need to buy special pots, pans, utensils, etc. for your camping. Similar to the first aid kit, you likely already have extra items around the house that will never be missed. Even if you don't, you can go to your nearest thrift store and buy used items for next to nothing and then not worry about how much you dirty them up while camping. You should be able to outfit your camping box for under $30.

When you consider that the cost of these cooking items, plus a marginal amount for food ingredients, is less than the cost of two or three family meals at a restaurant, that means you're getting a complete payback on your investment in less than a day, and it may even taste better than restaurant food! And this is in addition to all the money you're already saving on lodging.

Comfort/Optional Items:
- Air Mattress. I've noticed that as I get older, my back agrees less and less with the hard ground, and a good inflatable air mattress has become almost a basic necessity, at least for longer trips. Fortunately, it usually doesn't cost much—around $40 including the pump for a double size—and packs into a small space. Just make sure before your trip that the mattress will fit inside your tent!
- Cots. You will sacrifice some precious packing space for cots, but like the mattress, they offer the advantage of keeping you off the ground and, therefore, a little warmer, dryer, and comfortable. They start around $30.
- Lawn Chairs. Again, a big tradeoff with packing space for other things, but if your site doesn't come with a picnic table, or if you just want something more comfortable and flexible than a wood bench, you may opt for this "luxury".
- Camp Cookers/Pie Irons. These are so convenient and easy to pack that, if you already have them, I would almost move them up the list to Basics-II cooking gear. They resemble a single-serve waffle or burger maker on the end of a stick and you can use

them to cook a lot of different things, but the most common are probably grilled cheese sandwiches and, of course, pies. The only other thing you need is a fire and they have the added benefit of almost no dirty dishes or clean up. About $20 each.

- Dutch Oven. While I don't recommend Dutch oven cooking for beginner campers, if or when you want to give it a try, they start around $30–$40 for four- or five-quart cast-iron models. Remember, they are cast iron and very heavy (12–17 pounds), something to consider for when you're hauling gear from the car to the campsite.

Packing

True story: I took a family of two adults, five kids (including a toddler), a small dog, and all our gear and food on a five-day camping trip in a seven-passenger minivan. And we didn't store any gear on the roof. That's right. How did we do it? We had all the items in Basics-I and II, and even a few comfort items like an inflatable air mattress. But we just focused on the essentials and trimmed all the other nice-to-have items off our list.

Many people have the mistaken idea that the only way they can haul all their camping equipment, food, etc. is to use a large SUV, trailer, pickup truck, or full-size van. Some people even rent large vehicles just to go camping, violating both the simple and cheap principles. While there may be some extreme examples where this is necessary, you should instead focus on what your existing vehicle can accommodate and then adjust your camping equipment as needed to fit the car, not the other way around.

Now, what if you happen to run out of space in your vehicle before finishing packing the Basics-I and II, or you absolutely, positively, must take a few more optional/comfort items? Before giving up, or renting a larger vehicle, I recommend trying one of the handy, car-top cargo carriers. They come in both hard and soft-cover varieties and start around $50. The soft-cover carriers are usually cheaper and can be flattened and stored more easily when not in use. Besides the extra cost, the downside of any car-top cargo carrier is the extra wind resistance, which will cost you a few miles per gallon in fuel economy. But if it allows you to fit in those last few cots or lawn chairs, you may decide it's worth the cost and you're still far ahead in total savings compared with traditional lodging.

CHAPTER FIVE
Food and Meal Planning

OF COURSE, IT'S POSSIBLE to have a good camping experience just enjoying the campfire and natural surroundings while relying on local restaurants, bakeries, and convenience stores for most of your meals. That's why food and cooking supplies are not listed as an absolute necessity when making tradeoffs for space in your vehicle. If that's what it takes to get you out camping at first, go for it and ease into the cooking part gradually.

However, if you have the space for the gear and want to save a lot of extra money, especially on extended trips, I recommend preparing and cooking at least one meal a day at the campsite. Some campgrounds will not allow fires and others may be short on firewood; still, in other cases you may not want to build a fire for more than one meal or wait for the coals of the fire to get ready for cooking, so that's why I recommend taking a camp stove even if you're permitted to build a fire at your campsite.

Unless you're a gourmet chef, the meals on your campout, like everything else in this book, should be kept simple and cheap, and planning kept to a minimum. When planning your trip, simply list out on a piece of paper two to three meals a day and the ingredients and cooking supplies required to make them. Then, the day before you leave, purchase the non-perishable items, assuming they're cheaper near home than where you're going. Some tips for meal planning:

- Keep it simple. Plan meals that are easy and fast to prepare, and easy and fast to clean up, leaving few dirty dishes. Especially if you're new to camping, don't attempt fancy, seven course meals, or time-consuming Dutch oven dinners on your first trip. Stick with the simple favorites at first, such as foil dinners, hot dogs, soups, stews, or other one-pan meals, expanding your menu as you get more experienced. Simple meals are also easier to do right the first time and avoid the challenge of keeping multiple foods warm at the same time. And if you have children, they will usually prefer the simple meals anyway.

- Keep everything flexible. Recognize that some days you may be visiting attractions away from your campsite and it may be more practical to prepare simple sandwiches beforehand or stop at a convenience store or restaurant. Years ago, our family was on a camping trip that included a night at O.L. Kipp State Park in Minnesota. It was September and as we approached the park, we drove past acres and acres of corn. We knew it was past harvest season and were surprised to see so many ears left on the stalks. When checking in, we asked the ranger about it and she suggested we help ourselves. We put our other meal plans on hold and had fresh corn over the fire that night.

- Plan some "fast" food. Some days you may get busy or not feel like making a time-consuming meal, so plan at least a few meals that are really fast and don't require a fire.

- Avoid meals that require packing perishable items. It will be hard to keep them fresh, even with a cooler. The best way I've found to have meals with fresh ingredients and still keep it simple, is either to plan those meals for the first day of the trip, or schedule time during your trip to find a supermarket nearby and shop for the ingredients the same day of the meal. One advantage of the second approach is it may actually make it unnecessary to pack a cooler, saving a lot of packing space.

The meal suggestions listed below are only a small sample of popular and easy camping meals. You can find many more in other books or online. Most of these can be prepared either on a camp stove or over the fire, and in some cases require only boiling water, or no cooking at all.

Breakfast – Easy and Quick, with No Cooking
- Cold Cereal and Milk
- Fresh or Dried Fruit

- Donuts and Danish

Breakfast – Requires Boiling Water or Cooking on Stove or Over the Fire
- Boiled Eggs
- Hot Instant Cereal
- Hot Cocoa
- Griddle Food (Pancakes, French Toast, Eggs, Bacon, Sausage, Hashbrowns)

Lunch
- Peanut Butter and Jelly Sandwiches
- Cold Cuts
- Snack Bars
- Canned or Powdered Soups/Stews
- Powdered Drinks

Easy Dinners – Over or In the Fire
- Foil Dinner. Most people have heard of this very popular and easy dinner, which also has the benefit of requiring no dishwashing or clean up (just throw the foil in the trash). There are countless variations on the common theme of placing some meat and vegetables in a foil pouch, placing it on hot coals, and simply waiting for 20–30 minutes, with occasional turning.

The basic recipe is this: prepare two sheets of aluminum foil, shiny side up (facing the food), three times the width of the food (or about fourteen inches). It should be large enough to go around the food and allow for crimping the edges for a tight seal. A clever trick to prevent scorching is to sandwich a wet piece of newspaper or paper towels between the foil sheets. Place on the foil some hamburger, thinly sliced potatoes, carrots, and onions. Keep the carrots cut very small so they'll cook thoroughly. Season with butter, salt, and pepper. Finish the package by making what's known as a drug store fold: bring the long ends of the foil together above your food, fold the edges over several times and crimp the edges to make a seal. Then roll or fold the remaining ends of the foil several times towards the middle, making a similar seal. You want to leave a little space in the foil for expansion, but also want it wrapped tight enough to avoid leaking or falling apart in the fire. Throw it on the coals for ten to fifteen minutes each side (depending on intensity of the coals), then check to see if it's done.

The variations on this are endless, and I won't attempt to list them, but many great ideas can be found in camping books and Web sites. Popular options include substituting for the hamburger other meats such as stew meat, chicken, ham, seafood, or even eggs and sausage; adding other vegetables, and modifying the seasoning with BBQ sauce, soy sauce, steak sauce, cream of mushroom soup, or other flavorings.

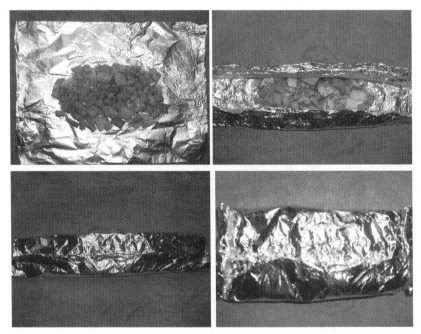

Foil dinner

- Weenies on a stick. Self explanatory. Easy, fast, and minimal cleanup.
- Hamburgers. Easy, fast and minimal cleanup. If the campsite does not come with an attached grill, this would require your positioning a grill over the fire, such as a collapsible grill listed in the camping box.
- Kabobs. Very easy, fast, and minimal cleanup. You can use metal or disposable wooden skewers with a combination of beef, chicken, or other meat, onions, peppers, mushrooms, etc. Carrots and potatoes are also good, but will require more cooking time. After assembling the food on the skewers, you can hold it over the fire (hot dog style) or cook on a grill.

- Camp Cooker/Pie Iron Meals. These are perfect for grilled cheese sandwiches: simply rub some butter on the inside of the iron to prevent sticking, insert the bread and cheese, close and hold over the fire for a few minutes. Variations include using real dough instead of bread, adding sauce and pepperoni to make pizza, and using pie filling to make dessert. It's easy, fast, and has almost no clean up.
- Fry bread on a stick. Just what it says – wrap some instant dough around a weenie stick and cook over the fire.
- Fresh Corn on the Cob. In addition to traditional boiling, you can also cook corn on the cob (husked) on a grill over the fire, or in a foil dinner. Or if you're feeling more adventurous, try leaving the husk on, soaking in water for a few minutes, and throwing into the coals for ten minutes, turning occasionally. Trust me, I've tried this last one and it works great.
- Fresh Baked Potato. Similar to corn on the cob, you can cook in foil or (and I dare you to try this) wrap it in mud and throw it in the coals for twenty minutes (you didn't plan on eating the skin anyway, did you?).
- S'mores. Self explanatory.

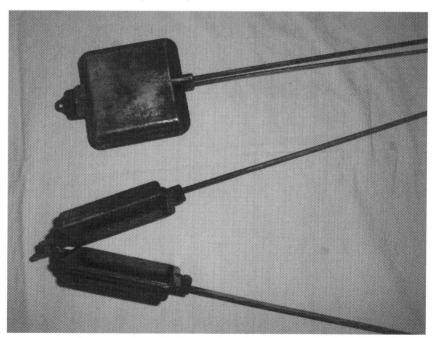

Camp cookers or "pie irons"

Easy Dinners in a Pan Over the Fire or On a Camp Stove
- Ziploc Boiled Dinners. This is a twist on the foil dinner, except insert the ingredients in a Ziploc bag and boil.
- Canned or Powdered Soups/Stews/Pasta/Potatoes. Very fast and easy. Will require some cleanup, but usually only dirties one pan.
- Dry Packaged Dinners and Instant Noodles/Ramen. Fast and easy, using boiling water and with minimal cleanup. If you use the instant noodles in a cup, you can even avoid a dirty bowl.

Dutch Ovens
Some people are literally evangelical in their enthusiasm for Dutch ovens, collecting and cataloguing their recipes, and hauling them around wherever they go. A Dutch oven is simply a cast iron pot that conducts heat very evenly and efficiently, allowing for many Crockpot or casserole-type dishes using just campfire coals. You generally place hot coals under and on top of the pot and then just wait for 45–60 minutes. They're popular for stews, lasagna, casseroles, cobblers, etc. Besides the weight and space they take up, their downside is that they are probably the most time-consuming camp meal you can make, requiring time for the fire to heat up and then almost another hour for the food to cook, but if you start early, that shouldn't be a problem. Also, if you're new to Dutch oven cooking, I strongly recommend not trying it on your first camping trip; or, if you do give it a try, have a backup plan for dinner. Otherwise, you may realize late at night that your little experiment was a disaster, you're still hungry, and you have nothing else to eat.

Dutch oven

CHAPTER SIX
Making Camp

What to Expect Upon Arrival at the Campground
If you've been camping before, you can probably skip this part, but it's worth mentioning a few things about what the novice camper can expect when arriving at the typical state or national park campground. Whether you have a reservation or not, you'll usually need to check in at a park office, typically right at the entrance to the campground. However, after hours, off-season, or at some less-visited campgrounds, the park may be operating on an honor system and just have some envelopes at the gate to record your campsite number and deposit your fee. In other cases, there may be instructions at the gate simply to proceed to select an available site and a ranger will visit your site later in the evening to collect payment.

Selecting a Campsite
In wilderness areas without assigned campsites, select durable areas that will not be harmed by your presence. Don't camp under dead trees or limbs that might fall. Stay out of gullies or low spots that could flood. Stay away from lone trees, mountaintops or other areas at risk of lightning.

At organized campgrounds with assigned sites, if you have the luxury of a large selection of available sites, keep a few things in mind when selecting a site (assuming you're tent camping):

- If the campground wisely sets aside areas exclusively for tents, they will usually provide more peace and quiet and give you something in common with your neighbors.
- If the campground mixes tent and RV camping in the same area, make every effort to camp next to other tent campers. Or, if the campground offers a choice of sites with or without electrical hookups, choose the sites without hookups. This will help avoid being disturbed at all hours by a neighbor's generator, air conditioner, or even television set.
- Stay reasonably close to toilet and shower facilities, especially if you have small children, but far enough away to avoid the annoyance of the lights, traffic, and any septic smells.
- Avoid sites near busy roads or high foot traffic areas, such as near the main trail to the restrooms or water spigot.
- To maximize sunshine in the morning and shade in the afternoon hours, select areas with tall trees on the west side.
- Select grassy sites where possible. Grassy sites not only provide a softer sleeping surface, but they also make it easier to keep kids, pets, and your tent floor clean.
- Choose sites where you're confident you can get along with the neighboring campers (and they'll get along with you).

Starting a Campfire

Assuming your campground allows you to have an open fire, a campfire becomes a potential cooking source, a way to keep warm, and adds the perfect atmosphere to an evening. Starting a campfire might seem easy, especially to aspiring arsonists and the unfortunate people who accidentally burn down their homes, but I've seen so many people fail at lighting campfires that it's worth a little discussion. The main reason they fail is lack of patience; they're in a hurry to cook and eat, or get warm, or just enjoy the fire atmosphere, and so they take shortcuts and skip important steps in the fire-building process. If you simply rush to light any stray piece of wood, you'll very likely end up spending much more time later trying to resuscitate a poorly-made fire and re-laying and re-lighting several more times. So, besides remembering the matches, the most important requirement to start and enjoy a good campfire is patience. Follow these steps, in order:

- Select a spot for the fire. Most state and national parks will provide fire rings at the campground and will prohibit making fires anywhere else. If fires are allowed, but a pre-made fire ring or area is not provided, select an open area away from trees, brush, dry grasses and low-hanging branches and make a simple fire ring by positioning large stones or other fireproof objects in a circle to contain the fire.

If you must make your own fire area, keep it environmentally friendly by making it in a way that protects the organic soil. For example, it's recommended to select a spot on mineral soil, like gravel or sand. If that's not possible, you should either move some mineral soil from somewhere else to make a protective floor for the fire, or actually dig down several inches and remove the organic topsoil and make the fire in the pit. Then, when you're finished with the fire, you should return the mineral soil where you got it or replace the organic topsoil.

- Gather the fuel, which may include:
  - Tinder: small, dry sticks, leaves, grass, pine needles, shredded bark, anything that will catch fire immediately without any coaxing.
  - Kindling: dead twigs about the thickness of a pencil.
  - Fuel wood: the larger stuff that will burn awhile. Be aware of, and obey, any restrictions in your campground about gathering wood. It's prohibited in most places to cut down trees or limbs for fire wood. If you're not sure how much good, dry wood will be in the campground, it may be necessary to purchase and bring your own.

- Lay (or build) the fire. There are several popular ways to lay a fire, but the basic principles and goals are the same for each:
  - Layer from small, fast-burning to larger, slower-burning items.
  - Provide plenty of "breathing" room for the fire.
  - Start with a little newspaper rolled up in balls (fire-building purists will skip the newspaper, but this is a book about keeping it simple!).
  - Lay some of the smaller tinder over the newspaper.
  - Position some of the kindling sticks around the area in a way that maximizes air flow.

Be patient. Only after you've placed several layers with lots of breathing room are you ready to strike a match. Here are the most popular methods:

Tepee method. Lay the kindling sticks against each other around the tinder and paper area in a tepee-shape. Once it's started, continue to feed the fire with larger wood around the tepee.

Fire lay: Tepee method

Lean-to method. Similar to the tepee method, but instead of leaning the sticks against each other, lean them against a stable object, like a large rock or log. While the air flow may not be as good as the tepee method, the structure is more stable and less likely to collapse before the fire gets going.

Log cabin method. Lay the kindling sticks and larger wood horizontally in a box shape, enclosing the tinder and paper, alternating directions so there is plenty of air flow between the sticks.

Fire lay: Log cabin method

- Light the fire. Using a match or lighter, light the paper and tinder.
- Assist the air flow. Once you've got a flame, you will usually need to assist the airflow by bending down and blowing low into the core of the fire, like a bellows, to keep it going and to accelerate the larger wood catching fire. This is critical during the first five to ten minutes of the fire, before the paper and

tinder are consumed. Don't hesitate to get down on your hands and knees to focus the blowing. Depending on the dryness and type of kindling and wood, you may need to do this on and off for some time until the kindling and larger wood catch fire. I've found that waving an object like a paper plate or Frisbee can also work well.

- Add larger wood. As it slowly catches, be prepared to keep feeding it with more kindling and gradually the larger pieces of fuel wood.
- Wait. If you plan to cook on your fire, this is the other area where patience is required. Once the fire is burning on its own, you need to be prepared to wait 20–30 minutes for some good hot coals to form and for a stable, hot temperature to develop before cooking over or in the fire. It's worth the wait.

Keep Your Fire Clean

Most campgrounds will either provide trash bins or require you to carry out any of your trash. Some people will attempt to burn some of their trash in the fire, but keep in mind that metals, like cans and foil, and plastics will not burn and should not be thrown in the fire, or left in the fire ring. Other materials like foam cups may emit toxic fumes or may not be environmentally safe and should be not be burned. Before vacating your campsite, check to ensure you're not leaving behind any trash around the campsite or in the fire ring.

Putting Out the Fire

A discussion of campfires would not be complete without emphasizing the importance of extinguishing your fire when you're finished. Even if the fire appears to be out, hot coals can smolder at the bottom for many hours and, with a little wind, easily cause forest fires. If you carried your water into the campsite and no nearby water source is available, be sure to save some of your water to put out the fire at the end of each day. Douse the fire with water, stir, and douse again. A rule of thumb for determining when the fire is completely extinguished is that the area is cool enough that you could run your hands through the ashes without getting burned.

Cleaning the Fire Site

Finally, before leaving, make sure the fire site is at least as nice as you found it, preferably better. Remove and dispose of any foil, cans, or other materials that don't burn. If you created your own fire area or pit, replace any removed topsoil and return the ground to its original state.

CHAPTER SEVEN
Camping with Children and Pets

Camping with Children

Children are usually easier to convince to go camping than adults. They totally get into the adventure and romance of camping out and sitting around a campfire. We took our children camping with us throughout their childhood and never once did any of them say, "Can't we just stay in a hotel?" There's something about young minds that are attracted to the atmosphere and adventure of camping, but unfortunately, most people, especially girls, outgrow this quality sometime in the late teens. I can think of almost no downsides to taking children camping and, on the contrary, it provides opportunities for closeness and bonding not possible or likely at home or in traditional lodging. Here are a few tips for make camping with children more enjoyable. Interestingly, they're the same tips to spending quality time with the kids at home or in a hotel, but it's easier to make it work while camping.

- Take a few card games or other interactive activities. Avoid the temptation to take DVD's and video games. Force yourself to go low-tech and you'll notice more togetherness and conversation.
- For infants and toddlers, take a baby backpack. They're much more appropriate in a campground setting than a stroller. In fact, leave the stroller home unless you'll be going to a mall or museum or some other place on your trip with nice, smooth surfaces. Even then, use it around the campground or when walking on trails.

Baby backpack

- Plan food that the kids will like. This may seem obvious, but many kids won't care for that expensive steak you brought and will in fact prefer food like hot dogs and foil dinners.
- Slow down the travel pace. Camping normally forces you to do this anyway, but remember that kids may tire out earlier, or take more potty breaks, etc., so take your typical adult itinerary and cut it in half.
- When selecting a campsite, be sensitive that some neighboring campers may not appreciate kids as much as you do. Some people, in particular, get very irritated if babies cry, or kids cut through their campsite or use loud voices. If you think your neighbors fall into this category and it's too much trouble to move, make an extra effort to keep your kids out of their way.
- Crawling infants pose a particular challenge to keep clean in the natural dirt floor of a campsite. A grassy campsite, if available, helps solve this problem; or, if you're desperate and have the packing space, you may want to take along a portable playpen.
- Be aware, and be prepared, that children need much more supervision, especially around the fire. Infants and toddlers, like the rest of us, will be fascinated by the glowing fire and want to approach it. Older kids will inevitably want to insert or thrown branches and other things into the fire, conducting their own little hazardous experiments. This is part of the excitement of camping

41

and you don't want to outlaw everything and, realistically, you won't be able to; but one rule I've seen parents impose is that it's okay to put things *into* the fire, but never take anything back out. Also, because the campsite is an open area with no walls or fences, you will need to be alert to toddlers wandering off. One technique our family has used to avoid the situation where one person mistakenly thinks somebody else is watching the child, is to formally put one of the parents or older siblings in charge of watching the toddler for a set period of time.

• Savor the Experience. When our oldest son, Christer, was about seven years old, we took a long weekend camping trip to The Pinery Provincial Park in Ontario, Canada on the coast of Lake Huron. It was a beautiful area and, included in the camping fee, was a ranger-guided nature walk in the evening. When the program was over, it was well past sunset and, as most campers know, when it gets dark in a wilderness area, it really gets dark! We couldn't see more than a few feet in front of us and we had just one flashlight for the five of us, so we huddled close together as we walked the half mile or so on a wooded trail back to our campsite.

My son Christer was at that age when boys want to grow up and be brave and not show a hint of fear of the dark, or the forest, or the boy-eating wolves waiting at every bend. Boys at that age may show affection, such as hugging or holding hands, but may also find it embarrassing or a sign of weakness, especially when there are friends or siblings around. Meanwhile, as a typical father, I wanted him to be tough, but also treasure those huggy moments when he was younger. Needless to say, Christer had resisted exhibiting any kind of fear or dependence, but about halfway into our walk in the pitch black, he cleared his throat and said, "Dad, can I hold your hand?" "Of course", I replied. It remains as a very simple, yet poignant, memory of the trip. There will be plenty of other opportunities to be tough. When was the last time something special like that happened to you on the walk from the ice machine back to your hotel room?

Peeing in the Woods (and other transcendent experiences)
What is a kid's favorite part of camping? Most everyone would correctly guess that it's the campfire. There's something about sitting around the fire, throwing things in, conducting all sorts of pyrotechnic experiences that really gets kids excited. Okay, so what is their second favorite part? Well, for young

boys anyway, I learned this when my oldest two sons were about four and six years old. It's not the tent or the hiking or the food or the ghost stories or any of that. It's the opportunity to pee in the woods. You who have sons will know exactly what I'm talking about. There's something about that complete freedom to violate society's standards of hygiene and just go on a tree, even if (or especially if) there's a restroom nearby. I would occasionally find my sons wandering off together to experience this primitive thrill. Sometimes, just to make it a little more interesting (and educational), they would try to cross their streams and then, in unison, say "X's", describing the letter of the alphabet it resembled. I don't know if my wife ever saw this and if she did, she probably didn't appreciate it as much as a father could, but the fact that I'm writing about it years later shows it has a cute nostalgia to it. I'm fairly confident you don't see this very often in a hotel bathroom and it's just another example of the unique experiences you can have while camping.

Camping with Pets

One of the huge advantages of camping versus more modern lodging options is the freedom to take pets along. I recommend you check with the campground in advance, but most will allow this with certain restrictions, such as keeping them on a leash and not leaving them alone in the campground. Dogs love camping as much as kids (but with less whining and maintenance!). A few things to keep in mind when planning to take your dog or other pet:

- Be sure to bring a container of your pet's own food and water dish. It's often very difficult for dogs to drink while traveling or in the campground unless you can first pour water into a bowl.
- To help your pet feel more secure in a strange environment, and to avoid risky encounters with wild animals, keep it inside the tent with you at night. If you don't like the idea of your pet sleeping next to you, many family-size tents nowadays have separate little mudroom areas that are perfect for them. Some tents even have special pet entrances.
- Don't leave your pets alone in the campground.
- Don't leave your pets in a car for extended periods, especially on a hot day.
- Remember pets are susceptible to ticks. Be sure to check your pet for ticks.
- Some mushrooms and other wild plants are poisonous to pets. Keep your pet from touching or eating any plant you're not sure is safe, and contact your veterinarian immediately if you think your pet has eaten a poisonous plant.

Don't forget the dog!

Also, listed below are some common state or national park campground rules related to pets. I strongly recommend you check the rules before leaving on your trip to avoid surprises. You can usually find the rules on the park Web sites or in the literature as you enter the campground. Rules may vary by park: generally, the busier the park, the stricter the rules, so you may be able to avoid excessive pet rules by visiting less-crowded, more rural parks. Listed below are just examples of common rules related to pets; the parks you visit may be more or less strict:

- Pets are not allowed in the following places:
  - Buildings
  - Picnic areas and picnic shelters
  - Beaches, except designated "dogs allowed" beaches
  - Playgrounds
  - Marked nature trails
  - Cross-country ski trails when groomed for skiing
  - Observation towers
  - Indoor group camps and related facilities
- Pets must be on a leash no longer than eight feet at all times. Using a leash helps prevent your pet from bothering people,

especially people with other pets. Leashing your pet also can help you control what your pet can eat or drink, helping ensure its safety and health.

- Pets must be under control at all times. Pet owners are not allowed to let their pets interfere in any manner with other people's enjoyment of the park. Pet owners who fail to properly control a pet or whose pet creates a public nuisance or other disturbance may be asked to leave the park or may be issued citations. Leaving your pet unattended for periods of time is inconsiderate to other park users and exposes you to potential problems.

- Loose pets may be seized and are subject to local laws pertaining to stray animals. Owners of loose pets may be ticketed. If your pet is lost, inform a park ranger and immediately call the local authorities to find the location of the nearest stray-holding facility.

- Be careful when choosing where to tie your pet in the campsite, so that children or other visitors will not be frightened or bitten.

- Make sure your pet has a current rabies vaccination and an identification tag in case it is separated from you. If you travel often with your pet you may wish to buy your pet an additional identification tag that includes the number where somebody can be reached when you are not at home.

- Pet owners are responsible for proper removal and disposal of their pets' waste products. Waste should be disposed of in dumpsters or trash receptacles.

CHAPTER EIGHT
Camping Rules and Etiquette

IN A TYPICAL CAMPGROUND, strangers share an open area, absent of walls, fences, and other barriers that help keep them civilized. Fortunately, most campers are courteous, sensitive, and generally good neighbors. On the other hand, a few people think that semi-roughing it in a tent is license to discard all manners and restraint. To help keep the few offenders in check, most popular, organized campgrounds have their own sets of written rules and etiquette. Unfortunately, some campgrounds take this to the extreme and seem to be managed by the same people who run public swimming pools, with so many detailed and suppressive rules that you wonder what's left that *is* allowed.

At frequently visited state and national parks, the rangers have developed written rules based on years of experience and, even though some may seem strict or obscure, there's probably a good reason for them. Like with pets above, rules may vary dramatically by camping area. Generally, rules will be most strict at parks or nature areas that are very popular or busy, or ecologically-fragile. Here are some examples of common rules you may find:

Common Written Campground Rules
- Tents must be pitched only in tent areas.
- Maximum two vehicles per campsite.
- No washing dishes at fountains or public spigots.
- No loud music.
- No generators or air conditioners in tent camping areas.
- Quiet hours 11:00 PM to 6:00 AM, but some parks extend it to twenty-four hours.

- No skateboard, roller skates, or scooters.
- No cutting down trees.
- Pets must be on a leash at all times.
- Don't leave pets alone at the campsite.
- No dogs allowed on the beach.
- Fires must be in designated fire rings.
- Firewood restrictions – some parks will not allow campers to bring in wood unless it was purchased nearby; this is to protect against harmful insects.
- Don't feed the wildlife.

Other Rules Often Imposed by State and National Parks
- Restrictions or prohibitions relating to alcohol, fireworks, and hunting
- Rules against destroying, molesting, defacing, or removing any natural growth or natural or archaeological feature from the parks. However, you may be allowed to pick edible fruits, nuts, wild mushrooms, etc.
- Rules against collecting seeds from herbaceous plants such as grasses and wildflowers.
- Rules against collecting rocks, minerals or fossil materials on state natural areas, state wild rivers, state parks, state trails, state forest preserves, or state recreation areas.

Unwritten Rules
Now, NO CAMPGROUND WILL attempt to post written rules related to every possible dangerous or annoying behavior, so you should also consider a number of "unwritten" rules, which could include the following:

- Don't take long showers or occupy the restrooms for a long time.
- Don't monopolize the electrical plug outlets in the rest rooms.
- Don't engage in loud, obscene, profane, or drunken behavior.
- Keep kids (and dogs) close and well-behaved.
- Don't hang embarrassing things on your campsite clothesline.
- Don't idle your vehicle for extended periods.
- Leave your campsite cleaner than you found it.
- Avoid walking through other people's campsites.
- Just be a decent, courteous human being.

You could probably think of even more ways someone could disrupt your camping experience, so just consider that the Golden Rule applies and, if some behavior would bother you, it would probably bother someone else. Do unto other campers as you would have them do unto you.

CHAPTER NINE
Problems and Solutions

You may be saying, "This all makes camping sound incredibly fun, but camping can be a pain in the butt sometimes and that's why I don't go more often." This chapter will deal with the most common challenges people have when camping and how to overcome them. Actually, with a few exceptions, you shouldn't expect any more problems during a camping trip than you would get on a traditional vacation, but you should still be prepared for them. Here are some of the most common.

Hard Ground/Poor Quality Sleep
This is probably the number one complaint about camping from adults (for some reason, kids can sleep on cold concrete and never complain), but can usually be solved fairly easily. If your campground has a variety of sites, try to choose one that is on grass or a thick leaf cover. Also, if your sleeping pad does not give you enough cushion, I strongly recommend an air mattress or fold-up cot. Neither item takes up much space in the car and could very likely determine if you (especially women) ever go camping again, so if you think it will be an issue, play it safe and take them on your first trip, because otherwise there may never be a second one.

Bugs
Obviously you've already thought of taking repellent, but some people are simply disgusted by all the bugs flying around the camp, in the restrooms, in the tent, etc. This high level of intolerance is primarily a result of our modern, air-conditioned society. We quickly forget that years ago, before air conditioning, we kept the doors and windows open and, even with screens,

bugs would get in the house. When it got too hot inside, we went out on the patio or porch and I bet there were plenty of bugs out there too. There was less of a dividing line between "inside" and "outside" and they often just blended together. Sure, the bugs were annoying, but we learned to tolerate or ignore them. Besides repellent, in the evening, wear long sleeves, pants, and a cap, minimize the lights in camp, quickly dispose of food waste and garbage after meals, and you can use citronella candles and other remedies. But for the most part, just get over it! It may take a few outings to get used to it, but don't give up.

Dirt
Usually more of a problem for women than men. Unfortunately, I don't have much of a solution for this other than to try to encourage you by saying as you camp more, you'll get more tolerant and realize everybody else is just as dirty.

Annoying Neighbors
We pulled into a beautiful state park in Michigan and quickly set up camp, with plans to cook a great campfire meal, relax around the campfire, and enjoy the solitude of the woods. But then, They arrived. They screamed and shouted profanities at their kids in a voice I wouldn't use behind the walls of my own home. They kept their car idling for close to an hour while they unloaded, presumably to keep the battery charged while they cranked up the volume on the car stereo. Perhaps they thought that everyone else in the campground must have the same excellent taste in music and that we would be forever grateful that someone pulled into the campground to break the boring solitude, scare away the pesky wildlife, and liven up our camping experience with *Foghat's Greatest Hits*. When I asked the guy to turn down his stereo, he reluctantly agreed, but acted like I was violating his civil rights.

Fortunately, this was the exception in our camping experiences, but how should you handle it? If they are blatantly breaking written campground rules, you can go ask the ranger to talk to them, but I suggest first going over to meet them, striking up a conversation, and politely asking them to cool it. You may still have to go to the ranger or, worst case, move to a different site, but don't just sit and fume and be miserable. Sometimes the people who seem the most annoying at first can, once you meet them, end up being quite interesting. Or maybe not. But keep in mind that, unlike bad neighbors back at home, you'll only be next to them for a few nights and then you'll be gone. Slow ride, take it easy...

Annoying Animals

While most people will say watching wildlife is one of the most enjoyable parts of camping, they don't enjoy it when animals get into the food and destroy tomorrow's dinner. If you park the car near the campsite, the best way to resolve this is to lock your food in the car each night (however, don't do this if you're in bear country or they could damage your car). You can also make a "bear bag" – put your food in a bag, tie one end of a rope to it, throw the other end over a tree branch, and hoist the food up in the air, tie it off, and keep it there overnight or while you're away from camp for extended periods.

Bad Food

Poor-quality food is usually the result of poor planning (you forgot to bring ketchup for the hot dogs) or being in too big a hurry (you try to cook over a fire before it's had a chance to burn down to hot coals), or just monotony (hot dogs for four straight nights!). Plan your meals, keeping them simple but also including variety. Then at meal time, slow down and, like the French, make the meal part of the experience, not just something to do before you go somewhere else.

Broken Camping Gear

Years ago, my family was on a camping trip near Toronto one summer and we were excited to use a brand new dome tent. But when I unpacked the tent and started to assemble the poles, the elastic shock cords inside two of the pulls immediately broke. You can probably imagine that the cords are almost impossible to thread back through the poles to reattach. This was the only tent we had; what were we going to do? Stores now actually sell little repair kits for fixing this problem, which are actually based on the same remedy I came up. I found some fishing line, tied it to one end of the severed cord, threaded it through the pole, pulled the cord through until it reached the other severed end, and tied the two ends together. Problem solved. Now you know why fishing line was included in the camping box.

Minor Medical Problems

We've already mentioned the importance of taking a first aid kit, regardless of how short or long, or how civilized or primitive your trip is. You can't practically be prepared for every medical problem or discomfort, but here are the most common minor problems while camping or engaging in other outdoor activities, with recommended treatment for most items as described in the Boy Scout Handbook:

- Minor cuts and scratches. Wash wound with soap and water, apply antiseptic to prevent infection, and keep it clean with an adhesive bandage.
- Larger cuts and bleeding. Use direct pressure to stop bleeding; clean the wound, cover with sterile gauze or clean cloth folded into a pad, held in position with tape.
- Sunburn and other first-degree burns (mild burns without blisters). For sunburn, first prevent it by wearing sun-protective clothing, like a broad-brimmed hat, and applying sunscreen. Other first-degree burns include minor burns from the fire or cooking, or hot water scalds. In all cases, hold the burned area under cold water until there is little or no pain.
- Minor second-degree burns (with blisters). Hold the burned area under cold water, let it dry, then protect it with a sterile gauze pad, being careful not to break the blisters. Don't apply creams, ointments, or sprays. More severe burns (third-degree) require immediate professional medical attention.
- Ticks. Protect yourself by wearing long pants and a long-sleeved shirt. Inspect yourself (and your pets) daily. If a tick has attached itself, grasp it with tweezers close to the skin and gently pull until it comes loose, being careful not to leave parts of the tick in your skin. Wash the wound with soap and water, and apply antiseptic.
- Other minor bites and stings. These can usually be treated by simply cleaning the area and applying an over-the-counter anti-itch treatment.
- Skin rashes from plants. The sap from poison ivy, poison oak, and poison sumac must be on your skin for ten to twenty minutes before it causes problems, so if you think you've been exposed, immediately wash the area with soap and water. You may need to change and wash your clothing as well. Calamine lotion helps relieve the itching.
- Dehydration. Signs of dehydration may include fatigue, head and body aches, and confusion. Prevent dehydration by always carrying plenty of water with you on hikes and other activities, even in cooler weather. More serious heat-related conditions include heat exhaustion and heat stroke, which usually require immediate medical attention.
- Hypothermia. You can suffer from hypothermia even if the temperature is above freezing, such as while hiking in the wind and rain, or swimming in cool water. Symptoms include feeling

cold and numb, fatigue, anxiety, confusion and stumbling, uncontrollable shivering, and even loss of consciousness. Treatment includes finding shelter, changing into dry clothes, and warming up with blankets, fire, and drinking warm fluids. Seek medical care if needed.

- Food Poisoning. This may seem obvious, but the best way to prevent food poisoning while camping is to avoid eating or cooking with fresh meat or eggs on your trip unless you buy them shortly before cooking them. Even keeping food in an ice cooler is not always reliable during hot summer days. Also, don't drink from any streams or other water sources that are not clearly potable. Treatment primarily involves over-the-counter medicine for diarrhea and increased fluid intake to avoid dehydration. If symptoms become severe or last more than twenty-four hours, hospital treatment may be required.

Rain/Weather
See next chapter

CHAPTER TEN
Weather

MY FAMILY WAS ON a camping trip in northern Michigan and everything was going well until, as we headed toward beautiful Copper Harbor on the south shore of Lake Superior, we noticed storm clouds approaching. It was getting late in the evening and just as we pulled into the state park campground, it started to rain. We hurried and set up our tent before the rain got too heavy and were quite proud of ourselves for setting up our tent in record time and having a refuge from the increasing rain. We kept dinner simple and decided to retire for the evening and sleep through the rain. When I awoke the next morning, everything was wet – the floor, my clothes, the sleeping bag, you name it. Just as I was about to feel sorry for myself, I looked over at my oldest son, and was horrified to see that his head was actually resting in a puddle of water, while he was still sleeping! I thought, "How could this be?" We had a good tent and a good rain fly, and had not pitched the tent in a low area or ditch. Sure enough, the walls and ceiling were perfectly dry. On inspecting the tent outside, I realized that as the rain had fallen all night long, it landed on portions of the tarp that were poking out from underneath the tent beyond the cover of the rain fly, then channeled right under the tent between the tarp and the tent floor, and soaked into the tent through the floor. Never again. Never, never again.

Weather can make or break a camping trip. As humans, when we can't control our environment, the next best thing is to adapt to it, and weather is the great "uncontrollable". I'm not saying any camping trip can be salvaged into a great time regardless of the weather. A couple times, after three or four straight days of rain, I've thrown in the towel and reverted to Plan B for our family vacation.

Sometimes, extreme weather can actually enhance the trip and, while it may be temporarily scary or unpleasant, can create fond and exciting memories of your trip that you'll talk about long afterwards. During the hot season, for example, a short rain shower can actually be welcome and pleasant.

One of my most vivid memories of extreme weather during a camping trip was while my family was camping at Dinosaur National Monument in eastern Utah. It was September and, technically, the off-season, so there weren't very many other campers at the campground. After a hot day near one hundred degrees (38 Celsius), we were relieved for the cooler temperatures that the evening brought and when we settled in our tent for the night, the skies were clear and star-filled. In the middle of the night, however, we were awakened by some of the most violent thunder and lightning I had ever experienced. Interestingly, there was no rain, but the light and sound virtually knocked us out of our bags as sleep became the last thing on our minds. Our kids clutched their parents as we just lay there frozen for about an hour, alternating between terror and fascination, as this spectacular show in the sky progressed. Eventually, it passed and we went back to sleep, but that short, one-hour experience was forever burned into our memories of camping.

A little, temporary bad weather need not derail your camping trip. The key is to prepare for that temporary bad weather.

Rain
Rain is probably the most-feared event on a camping trip, particularly if it rains during the day and your trip includes lots of outdoor activities. Even with a favorable weather forecast, rain can hit anytime while camping, especially if you're camping in remote mountains or valleys where weather conditions can change very quickly. Regardless of the forecast, I recommend packing at least one extra pair of clothes, especially socks, to deal with the unexpected drenching.

For rain in the daytime, you should prepare a Plan B for your activities; instead of the beach, go to a lighthouse; instead of the hike, go to the nature center; instead of sitting around camp, go for a drive. Make sure everything at camp is covered and tight and just go somewhere indoors. The worst thing to do is to sit around getting wet and cold and miserable. If you have a tarp or kitchen rain fly, you can still cook and eat meals at your campsite during the rain. If you don't have any shelter like that, a rainy day might be the time to go out to a restaurant or a convenience store for lunch.

After retiring at night, if you're prepared, rain shouldn't really cause too many problems. In fact, it can actually be pleasant and relaxing to lie in your tent hearing the rain fall outside … as long as you're confident the rain will stay on the outside of the tent!

If you're expecting rain, here are some tips to keep the rain outside where it belongs.

- Be as selective as possible about the grade or slope of the tent site. Look for higher ground or areas in a mound shape (excluding anthills of course).
- Position the tarp or ground cloth correctly. You probably already know to use a tarp or ground cloth under your tent as a moisture barrier, but don't forget this critical lesson I learned above: fold and position the tarp so no part of it extends beyond the perimeter of the tent or rain fly. In fact, just make it a rule to position the tarp so you can't see any of it if you walk around the tent. VERY IMPORTANT. If this is the only part of this chapter you remember, it will save you a lot of problems. Another technique that almost guarantees you'll stay dry during the night is actually to put a tarp on the floor inside your tent.
- Stake the tent down, making the floor and walls as tight as possible. Tent stakes are not just to prevent your tent from blowing away in the wind. They also prevent water from puddling or seeping in anywhere.
- Position the rain fly correctly. Most tent walls are not waterproof. That's why tents come with a rain fly. However, the fly is most effective if you keep it pulled very tight and away from the tent walls. In heavy rain, a fly making contact with the tent wall can cause the wall to wick water in from the fly. Rather than just attaching the fly to the tent corner stakes, it's better to use rope or cords that come with some dome tents to actually stake the bottoms of the fly several feet away from the tent, or even tie it to a nearby tree.

If your tent or rain fly gets wet, try to dry it out before repacking it. This may mean throwing it in the trunk unpacked while you travel home or to your next campground. Besides the obvious comfort reasons for wanting a dry tent, letting it dry before repacking will help avoid mold from growing on it while in storage. If your tent is wet and you've got more traveling and camping ahead of you, pull into a laundromat and throw the tent in a dryer for a few minutes—but only for a few minutes, being careful you don't melt it.

Heat

In a counter-intuitive way, it's actually harder to stay comfortable in hot weather than in cold weather. Cold weather can be handled by a fire and a good sleeping bag, but it can be challenging to find a refuge from excessive hot weather, unless you haul a portable air conditioner with you, but then you just violated both the simple and cheap principles. However, here are some practical things you can do:

- Sleep on top of your sleeping bag.
- Sleep outside of the tent.
- Where possible, pitch your tent near a stream.
- Keep the flaps and windows open on your tent to allow for ventilation.
- If no rain is in the forecast, don't attach the rain fly.

Cold

As mentioned above, a campfire and good sleeping bag can usually help you overcome the minor discomforts of cold weather.

Wind

Similar to the advice for rainy weather, be sure to stake down the corners of the tent and make the floor and walls as tight as possible, preventing any pockets that can catch the wind like a sail.

CHAPTER ELEVEN
Activities and Entertainment

MOST PEOPLE DON'T NEED advice on what kinds of fun activities to do while camping. In fact, if you're like me and my family, we usually select the location and activities we want to do first and then use camping as an affordable means of enjoying them. However, if you need a starter list, here it is:

Beaches
Many state parks offer campsites either on or near a lake or ocean beach. The great thing about camping near a beach is that, unlike typical daytrips, you can experience the beach at all times of the day or night—sunrise, sunset, or even under moonlight in the middle of the night. It gives you a whole new perspective on the beach.

Biking
Bicycling has become really popular recently and almost inseparable from camping in the minds of some people. On a recent camping trip to the Door County peninsula in Wisconsin, it seemed like almost every camping family brought bicycles with them and, for those few who didn't bring their own, rentals were available both inside and outside the state park.

Fun at the beach

Hiking

I'm not talking about twenty-mile wilderness treks, although you can do that if you're up to it, but rather whatever you and your party can handle and will enjoy. "Walking" may be a more accurate term. Use the lowest-common-denominator (LCD) approach: choose the hike appropriate for the least able of your group—usually the youngest or oldest person. If you're not sure what you're capable of, or if you haven't hiked more than a few miles for a long time, I recommend starting with short walks on marked trails. Most state and national parks will have a ready list of popular hiking trails of varying distances. Often the best trails start just a few minutes from your campsite. Be sensitive to the elevation rise of the trail—what appears on paper to be an easy two-mile walk could in fact be a strenuous two-mile climb. Even for short hikes, always take along a day pack, with some water bottles, a few snacks, a compass, cell phone, and a little money (just in case). Don't overdo it (keep it simple), but still be prepared.

Fishing

Libraries of books have been written on fishing, so I won't attempt to add anything here, other than you probably know somebody who would be perfectly content spending an entire camping trip just dropping a line in the water.

Orienteering

This is an educational game that involves setting up and following courses or treasure hunts using a compass. First, design a course with different waypoints, directions, and distances. Plant clues at each waypoint to get the person to the next waypoint, and so on. For example, a clue could read "walk 100 paces on a 140-degree bearing, where you'll find your next clue." The seeker is rewarded with a treasure at the final waypoint. Don't worry if you have no idea how to use a compass. A simple scout book or online resource could teach you the basics in under an hour, and then you will have learned a valuable survival skill as well.

GPS Games, Geocaching, and Earthcaching

In a similar but more high-tech version of orienteering, handheld global positioning satellite (GPS) devices can be used for treasure-hunting and other camping games. You can keep it simple and just play games around your campground similar to the compass games mentioned above, except using GPS coordinates for your clues.

Or, you can get more sophisticated and join the global online geocache community. Geocaching is a relatively new pastime where you use your GPS device either to hide or locate containers, called geocaches, and then share your experiences online. For example, if you're hiding geocaches, you might leave little notes or treasures in a water-proof container, hide it, and then post its GPS coordinates on any number of geocache Web sites so others can search for it. If you're searching for an item hidden by somebody else, you simply search the same Web sites for the coordinates of geocaches hidden nearby and then try to find them with your GPS device. Once you find the geocache, you're generally encouraged to sign a logbook and replace anything you take from the container with something of equal value. It's possible, if you're really into this as a hobby, to plan an entire camping trip around geocaching, researching treasure spots as you plan the trip, and then spending the trip searching for them and hiding some of your own.

Another activity similar to geocaching is earthcaching, but instead of finding human-placed items, you seek out natural features and landforms.

Bird/Plant/Animal Watching

Many state and national park campgrounds will have nature centers or literature available describing local flora and fauna, but if you want to make this part of your camping trip, I encourage you to invest in several good guide books.

Nature and Ranger Programs

Many state and national park campgrounds have nature centers with exhibits, video presentations, and literature on the local flora, fauna, culture, geography, and geology. Most campgrounds also include a number of outdoor programs free of charge, such as nature walks and campfire stories. Try not to let yourself get so busy visiting attractions outside the park that you miss these free programs often just steps from your campsite.

Photography

You don't have to be an experienced photographer with expensive equipment to enjoy photography. Most of the quality in a photo is in the composition, not the lens or megapixels, so take your $30 camera and document your trip. And don't skimp on photos of the people with whom you're sharing the trip. Some of my favorite photos are not of the historic lighthouse or impressive waterfall, but rather are photos of my family and friends on the trail, at the beach, in the canoe, or just hanging around the campsite.

Games

In a traditional hotel vacation, it seems the lights are always on and activities are continually dangled in front of you until late into the night. Your idea of a family activity often ends up passively watching the same television programs you're trying to get away from, with little or no communication. When camping, however, something about the involuntary darkness and self-imposed leisure time encourage you to do something different and more socially interactive. My suggested rules for games while camping are: 1) Keep it small – usually something that doesn't require much space or a well-lit area; 2) Keep it fast-paced; and 3) Keep the rules simple, especially if children are playing. Here are some of the most popular.

- Playing Cards. Our favorites are Uno and The Great Dalmuti (or you may know it as Crud, Scum, or President), but any games using custom or standard playing cards.
- Parlor Games, such as Charades and Pictionary
- Twenty Questions. Try variations for older kids, such as popular movies or songs.
- The Continuing Story, or What Happens Next. This simply begins by somebody starting a story ("there once was a boy and a dog...") and stopping after a few sentences. The next person must then continue the story for a few more sentences, free to

branch off into any number of storylines, and so on, continuing regardless of how ridiculous the story becomes.

- Campfire Storytelling or Circle Games. Although these work best with groups larger than the typical family, I'll mention them here anyway because you never know when you might be able to gather campers from several sites together for a game. There are many Web sites and books describing great games, so I'll only describe a few of the more popular ones:

I Took a Trip. Everyone sits in a circle and the leader goes around saying to each other player, "I took a trip. What did I take along?" When asked, each player then must name an object. The leader then goes around and asks a different question, but each player must give the same answer they gave before. The leader tries to ask questions that will make their answers seem more and more ridiculous, with the goal of causing other players to laugh. Anyone who starts laughing is out of the game. Last player to break up laughing wins.

Wink Murder. Everyone sits in a circle and the "murderer" is secretly selected, such as by drawing marked pieces of paper from a hat, so only the murderer knows who he is. Then everyone starts the game by sitting still and looking around the circle. When the murderer winks at anyone in the circle (and they realize it), they must scream and slump in their chair and "die" without disclosing the murderer's identity. If someone thinks they know who the murderer is, they accuse him. If wrong, the accuser dies and the game continues until the murderer is identified.

Two Truths and a Lie. This can be played around the fire or at a table. Each player takes turns telling three statements about himself—two that are true and one that's a lie. Everyone else then tries to figure out which statements are true and which are lies. Player or players with the most correct guesses wins.

- Traditional Sports and Field Games. These include games like football, baseball, Frisbee, and ultimate Frisbee.

- Capture the Flag. This is a mainstay of Boy Scout outings and, although best with eight or more players, it can be played with as few as six. The basic rules are:

Divide into two teams of three or more people each. Determine the playing field, boundaries, and border between adjacent territories for each team, using streets, trails, creeks, fence lines, etc. The field does not need to be square or symmetrical, but simply must have boundaries and a midfield borderline separating the two teams' territories. Select something, such as a towel, to use as a flag for each team. Each team goes to its territory and hides its flag anywhere, but it must be at head height and visible from twenty yards away.

Team members are safe while in their own territory. Members of each team attempt to sneak across the border into enemy territory, find and capture (take) the enemy flag, and then race back to their own territory without being caught. Defenders on each team try to intercept and capture (tag) any opposing players who sneak across to their territory. When captured, the prisoner must go to a designated prison in the defender's territory and can only be freed if tagged by a teammate and then successfully returns to his territory without being tagged again.

Win by capturing the enemy flag and carrying it back to your side of the border without being captured.

CHAPTER TWELVE
Off-Season Camping

When most people think of camping, assuming they even decide to go, they usually limit their trip dates to sometime between the Memorial Day and Labor Day holidays. This is consistent with most traditional vacations as well and is easy to understand given that in many parts of the country the weather is best during that period and also because the kids are on school break. Personally, this is also my favorite time to go. However, it doesn't have to be the *only* time you go camping. There are many benefits of taking one-day or longer camping trips in early spring, late fall, and, yes, even in the middle of the winter. Many state and national parks stay open year-round despite colder temperatures. Benefits include:

- No crowds. In the same way that it often pays to buy a stock when everybody else is selling, if you camp in the off-season, you'll have almost no competition for prime campsites and should never need to make a reservation.
- Camp fees are often reduced or even free, making it even cheaper than the already-cheap option of going in the summer.
- Campfire restrictions are eased because there is not as much risk of forest fires.
- The campfire feels great and warm camp food tastes even better when it's a little brisk outside.

- Winter camping can also be combined with activities only available during that season, such as cross country skiing, snowshoeing, ice fishing, snowmobiling, and seasonal wildlife watching.

In fairness, I must also mention the downsides of off-season camping:

- Some campgrounds can get muddy.
- Often the parks will shut off the water and you must bring your own.
- Other services and facilities may be shut down or have limited hours.

Snow camping

Years ago, our family took a short camping trip to a popular area during a weekend in November. We selected a campground we knew would be open which was literally on the top of a mountain and were a little concerned the temperatures dipping as low as forty degrees Fahrenheit (4 Celsius) during the night might make it difficult to enjoy the experience, but we figured, "what's the worst that can happen? If we have one bad night, we'll just pack up and go home, or to a hotel." Upon arriving in early evening, we quickly realized we were the ONLY people in the whole campground besides the manager and his wife. Seeming stunned that anybody had come that night, they directed us to an open area where we set up camp and ended up having a great evening, with fire, a nice meal, a game of Capture the Flag, and a great night's sleep. We had some friends who were staying a few miles away at more traditional lodging and paying traditional fees and we thought they were really missing out.

I've since been camping during every month of the year, including sleeping on top of two feet of snow in zero-degree (-18 Celsius) weather in January. Yes, it has its challenges, but also the benefits mentioned above. Two steps to making off-season camping enjoyable:

- Get a warm sleeping bag. You can't always trust sleeping bag temperature ratings, so I recommend getting one that's rated at least ten degrees lower than the expected low temperatures at the campsite. Just about every other piece of equipment can be the same as summer camping, but the sleeping bag is critical.
- Have a Plan B or plan of retreat, just in case everything goes wrong (blizzard, high winds, etc.). You would want to do this for regular season camping too, but it's even more important during off-season when you may not have any park rangers or others nearby to assist you if something goes wrong.

CHAPTER THIRTEEN
Backpacking/Canoeing Camping

THIS BOOK IS FOCUSED on camping that is Simple and Cheap, and backpacking or canoe camping may violate the cheap principle if it requires you to invest in a lot more equipment, or may violate the simple principle if it requires a lot more planning; but once you are comfortable with so-called auto-camping, you may want to give backpacking or canoe camping a try. It takes the concept of planning and careful packing to a whole new level. Instead of assuming you can stop and buy anything you forgot, you need to be thorough and expect you only have one chance to get it right. Instead of just trying to fit all your gear, clothes and food in a car, you're now trying to fit it all in a backpack and still keep it light enough to carry for long distances. Instead of relying on local supermarkets for ingredients for your next meal, you may need to pack all the food you need for the whole trip. But if done right, backpacking can open up whole new vistas of camping, allowing you to get off the beaten path, have more privacy, see more wildlife, test new skills in orienteering, cooking, etc.

If you're ready to tackle backpacking or canoe camping, you should plan a graduated approach—start out with simple, one or two-night trips, with short distances (less than five miles of hiking or canoeing) in familiar territory. Use these trips as a testing and proving ground for longer trips later. For example, on your first couple backpacking trips, you'll quickly learn how well your backpack fits, how much weight you can comfortably carry, how well your shoes and other clothing perform, and how quickly you get fatigued, sore, or dehydrated. You'll learn which members of your group or family need a little extra help. You'll also learn that some of the things you packed were never used and just added unnecessary weight, or that you failed to pack some critical items. With a canoe trip, you'll quickly learn how your body handles hours of paddling and how well you waterproofed everything.

Here's a list of the most common equipment you will need for backpacking:

- Backpack. These normally come in two types, external frame and the more common internal frame. Either one works fine. External frame has the advantage of being more versatile, with many places on the outside to attach gear. Internal frame has the advantage of being more comfortable and compact and, therefore, more maneuverable. The backpack may be the biggest investment in backpacking and can run over $100.

Internal-frame backpack

- Tent or Tarp/Rope/Stakes. The tent will often be the heaviest thing in your backpack. No need to spend a lot on fancy models, but you'll want to take the smallest, lightest one you can afford. Stick to one, two, or three-person tents. Backpacking is no place for a large, heavy six-person tent. To avoid one person getting overburdened carrying the tent, you can consider splitting it up and having one person carry some or all of the tent poles while another carries the rest of the tent. If you still find the tent takes up too much space or weighs too much, depending on where you're going, you can always choose to leave the tent home altogether and plan to sleep under the stars, taking a tarp and rope to fashion an emergency shelter between trees if needed. Backpacking is often a game of tradeoffs like this between convenience and space or weight.
- Sleeping Bag and Pad. Again, stick with as lightweight and small volume as possible, but there's no need to spend a lot of money unless you're expecting subfreezing temperatures.
- Trash Bag. This serves two purposes. First, most backcountry areas have no trash containers (are you surprised?) and you will be required to carry out all cans, plastic, and other trash. Also, a heavy-duty trash bag can serve as an emergency large poncho that will cover both you and your backpack if it rains.
- Rain poncho
- Small portable one-burner stove and fuel
- Pocketknife
- Mess Kit
- Basic utensils (that are not already included in your pocketknife
- Frypan. This is optional, but if you don't mind a little extra weight, it's highly recommended. I've found that the typical mess kit does a terrible job of distributing heat and when you try to use it as a frypan, food doesn't cook evenly and scorches.
- Matches/Lighter
- Food. For obvious weight reasons, you'll want to focus on dehydrated food, but if you don't mind a little extra weight, it's nice to pack one or two canned dinners to relieve the monotony and high cost of dehydrated food.
- Water. If your destination doesn't have a reliable water source, you'll have to carry in all your water, which dramatically adds to your backpack weight, but you'll need it for drinking and for rehydrating your food.

- Water purifier or purification tablets. If your destination does have a natural water source, you'll need a way to purify water, unless you're prepared to boil everything you eat or drink.
- Clothing and cap. Be prepared for both temperature extremes, but keep to absolute minimum. Every additional item adds more weight and takes up more space.
- Toilet Paper
- First Aid Kit, Toiletries, Bug Spray, Sunscreen
- Book
- Compass
- Camera
- Playing Cards or card games

Single-burner mini-stove

For canoe camping trips, the list is similar, except pay extra attention to waterproofing your gear. You are guaranteed to have water sloshing around in the canoe and, quite possibly, at some point you will swamp the canoe and all your gear will be in the water. Usually sealing up critical gear like tents, sleeping bags, clothing, and food in heavy-duty trash bags will do the trick.

I learned an important lesson about minimizing what you take backpacking when I lived in Indonesia and went on a backpacking trip with a boy scout troop in the remote Ujung Kulon National Park on the island of Java. Indonesia is near the equator, meaning it is always very hot and humid. We were backpacking seven to eight hours every day in dense jungle and I found myself getting very hot and exhausted carrying a fifty-pound backpack. A good portion of the weight in my pack was my tent and sleeping bag, but I soon realized that we were always camping near trees and it was always so incredibly hot at night that I slept on top of the sleeping bag. Conclusion: I ended up wishing I had left both the tent and sleeping bag home and instead packed only a sleeping pad, tarp, rope, and mosquito netting to cover basic shelter and bedding needs.

When you start considering the many tradeoffs between sleeping and cooking convenience versus the weight of your backpack, you might be surprised at what you decide to leave home.

Conclusion

WE HEADED WEST ON I-90 after a couple fascinating days and nights camping and hiking in Badlands National Park in the southern part of South Dakota. Our next stop was Custer State Park, an area we had never visited before, but selected because, like many of our camping trips, of its proximity to other famous or interesting sites. Custer State Park is just south of Rapid City, in the southwest corner of the state, within easy driving distance of Mount Rushmore and the Crazy Horse Memorial, and also just a few hours from Devil's Tower in northeastern Wyoming. We soon realized, however, that this state park would have much more to offer than just getting us close to these famous sites.

The park itself lies within the Black Hills National Forest, one of the most beautiful areas in the country, and includes the incredibly scenic Needles Highway (SD 87) with its famous corkscrew turns, tunnels, pig-tail bridges, and granite cliffs. And, if that's not enough, the park also features a wildlife loop through a preserve including herds of bison, mountain sheep, elk, and other large wildlife. As we read through the brochures obtained at the check-in area, we got more and more excited about this place. Convinced it couldn't get any better, we then proceeded to our campsite and selected a site that could have been on a picture-postcard. It was heavily wooded, quiet with lots of space between sites, and next to a small, scenic lake.

In our many years of camping in many different areas, we had experienced the good and the bad, the pretty and the plain, and I had become the camping equivalent of a restaurant critic—always on the lookout for that perfect balance of beauty, solitude, and activities. But like a restaurant critic, the more I experienced, the more demanding my tastes became, and I started to wonder if the so-called "perfect" camping trip was just an elusive dream. However, as we started to unpack our gear and set up camp at this site ... at least for that moment ... I thought we had found it.

About the Author

PAT SMITH IS AN active outdoor enthusiast, enjoying biking, running, hiking, and, of course, camping. He has been a regular camper with his wife and five children for over twenty-five years and a volunteer leader for the Boy Scouts of America for over ten years. He has camped in over twenty different states and four foreign countries, almost always keeping it simple and cheap, in a tent. His experience includes both leisurely auto-camping and "roughing it"-style backpacking and canoe camping; and he has camped in many state, provincial, and national parks, as well as private and wilderness areas. With a family of seven, plus a dog, he has tested the limits of packing a minivan and learned the secrets of how to keep spouse, kids, and pets happy while camping. Born and raised in northern Utah, he now lives in the Chicago area with his wife, Christine, and children.

Appendix

The Basics-I: Getting Through the Night

- Ground Cloth
- Tent
- Sleeping Bags and Sleeping Pads
- Clothes
- Hat or Cap
- Rain Jacket or Poncho
- Personal Hygiene/Grooming (soap, toothbrush, etc.)
- Towel
- Camera
- Day Pack
- Water Bottle
- Baby/Toddler Backpack (if you have very small children)
- First Aid Kit
- Bug Spray
- Sunscreen
- Pocketknife
- Flashlight
- Matches/Lighter
- Newspaper
- Tissue
- Hatchet or Saw

The Basics-II: Cooking, Eating, and Miscellaneous

- Stove and Fuel
- Food for one or two days
- Water (if not available in the campground)
- Camping Box, which includes:
  - Large Saucepan and Lid
  - Small Saucepan and Lid
  - Frypan or Griddle
  - Paper Towels
  - Ziploc Bags

- Aluminum Foil
- Large Spoon
- Kabob Sticks/Weenie Sticks
- Vegetable Oil
- Dish Soap
- Sanitary Wipes or Hand Sanitizer
- Sponge/Pad
- Dish Towel
- Pencil/Paper
- Salt & Pepper
- Extra Matches/Lighter
- Tongs
- Spatula/Turner
- Can Opener (or pocketknife)
- Kitchen Knife
- Potato Peeler
- Cutting Board
- Utensils
- Cups
- Bowls
- Plates
- Garbage Bag
- Duct Tape
- Bungee Cord
- Fishing Line
- Safety Pins and Needle/Thread
- Rope
- Collapsible Grill
- Hot Pad
- Pitcher/Water Container

Comfort and Convenience (space permitting)
- Air Mattress
- Cots
- Lawn Chairs
- Portable Playpen (for crawling babies)
- Camp Cookers/Pie Irons
- Dutch Oven
- Cooler and ice
- Card games and small sports equipment
- Reading Material

References

Boy Scout Handbook, The. Eleventh Edition. Irving, TX: Boy Scouts of America, 1998

Fieldbook. Third Edition. Irving, TX: Boy Scouts of America, 1984

Klinkenborg, Verlyn. "Our Vanishing Night." National Geographic, November 2008

Louv, Richard, *Last Child in the Woods.* Chapel Hill, NC: Algonquin Books of Chapel Hill, 2005

Index

—